Herbert Puchta & Jeff Stranks

G. Gerngross C. Holzmann P. Lewis-Jones

American MORE! ④

Student's Book

CAMBRIDGE
UNIVERSITY PRESS

HELBLING LANGUAGES

	Grammar	Language Focus and Vocabulary	Skills	MORE!
UNIT 1 Football!? Soccer!?	• simple present, present continuous, and present perfect (review)	• sports apparel **Sounds right** /s/ vs. /z/	• talk on the phone • buy things in a sporting goods store • read about unusual sports • listen to an American's trip to an Argentinian soccer game • talk and write about a memorable sports event	Learn **MORE** through English **Early U.S. history** **History**
UNIT 2 Space and beyond	• past continuous vs. simple past • past perfect • narrative tenses (review)	• travel	• give reasons • talk about your trip to school • listen and find out about *A race to space* • listen to a poem • talk about and write a short sci-fi story	**Check your progress** Units 1 and 2 Learn **MORE** about culture **Trains, planes, and automobiles!** Read **MORE** for pleasure **Far out**
UNIT 3 Shopping	• should(n't) / ought • gerunds	• money and shopping **Sounds right** spelling	• say what people ought to do • talk about shopping • read a quiz and talk about your shopping habits • read and listen to find out about Buy Nothing Day • write a letter to help someone with a money problem	Learn **MORE** through English **Space travel** **Science**
UNIT 4 A working life	• be going to / present continuous (review) • future time clauses	• personality adjectives	• say what you want to do • talk about personalities and jobs • read about a foreign girl living and working in the U.S. • listen to two people talking about their job interviews • write a description of someone's job	**Check your progress** Units 3 and 4 Learn **MORE** about culture **Park rangers** Read **MORE** for pleasure **Omelets and hard work**
UNIT 5 Bookworms	• so / such • phrasal verbs	• kinds of books **Sounds right** stress in compound nouns	• give reasons • talk about books • read about the Alex Rider books • listen to teens talking about reading • listen and talk and write about a book you enjoyed	Learn **MORE** through English **Migration** **Biology**
UNIT 6 The main event	• the passive • make / let / be allowed to	• special events	• talk about permission • talk about events • read about events in Rio de Janeiro • listen and talk about planning a charity event, then design a poster for it	**Check your progress** Units 5 and 6 Learn **MORE** about culture **Marathons!** Read **MORE** for pleasure **Chill out at Lollapalooza**

		Grammar	Language Focus and Vocabulary	Skills	MORE!
UNIT 7	**Food, glorious food**	• *will / won't* predictions • question tags (review)	• food **Sounds right** question intonation	• make offers • talk about food • read about a campaign for healthier food • talk about what food you like • listen to a radio report about the least healthy U.S. cities • write about your eating habits	Learn **MORE** through English **Musical styles** **Music**
UNIT 8	**Body talk**	• *could, might, may* for speculation • *-ed* vs. *-ing* adjectives	• body movements	• talk about emotions • talk about body movements • read about the history of body piercing • listen to a synopsis of the movie *Fantastic Voyage* • write a movie review	**Check your progress** Units 7 and 8 Learn **MORE** about culture **Street performers** Read **MORE** for pleasure **It must be her age**
UNIT 9	**Fame**	• *used to* (review) • gerunds after prepositions	• award shows **Sounds right** questions	• talk about past and present favorites • talk about awards • read about fame and happiness • listen to someone talk about their favorite star • talk and write about someone you admire • listen to the song *Fame*	Learn **MORE** through English **The city of Vancouver** **Geography**
UNIT 10	**Crazy collections**	• present perfect continuous • embedded questions	• hobbies and pastimes	• talk about collecting something • talk about hobbies • listen to someone talking about their collection • read about people with unusual collections • talk and write about collecting things	**Check your progress** Units 9 and 10 Learn **MORE** about culture **Unusual collections** Read **MORE** for pleasure **Museum of Dirt**
UNIT 11	**Speak out**	• reported speech • reported questions	• personality adjectives **Sounds right** reporting direct speech	• check what people do / explain what you do • describe people • read a poem • listen to teens talking about teens • talk about teenagers and their problems • read and write a letter to an advice page	Learn **MORE** through English **Understanding poetry** **English**
UNIT 12	**A fair world?**	• *if*-clauses (review)	• workplaces	• talk about what you would have done • talk about places • listen to stories about people who got into trouble • read a diary entry about an unfair situation and then write your own • discuss unfair situations and how you would react	**Check your progress** Units 11 and 12 Learn **MORE** about culture **Ethical buying!** Read **MORE** for pleasure **Fair? Well ...**

Wordlist

In this unit

You learn

- simple present (review)
- present continuous (review)
- present perfect (review)
- words for sporting apparel

and then you can

- talk on the phone
- buy things in a sporting goods store

1 **Listen and read.**

Emily	Juan! Hi. What are you doing here?	**Juan**	These are special gloves. You wear them when you play lacrosse. Have you heard of lacrosse?
Juan	Hi Emily. I'm waiting for Pete. We're going to the game together.	**Greg**	I think so. It's an old Native American game.
Emily	Oh, I see. By the way, this is my friend Greg.	**Juan**	That's right. I love it. I'm not very good, though.
Juan	Hey Greg. How are you?	**Emily**	It's a little like field hockey.
Greg	Hi Juan. Fine thanks, and you?	**Juan**	Well, it's not really, but never mind! So, Greg, do you play football?
Juan	I'm fine. So, you're not from around here, are you?		
Greg	No, I'm from Brazil. We live in Rio de Janeiro, but my dad's working in the U.S. for a year, so here I am.	**Greg**	Yes! I've played football since I was six years old. I'm a striker.
		Juan	A what? Hey, I get it. Sorry, I'm not talking about soccer, I'm talking about our football.
Emily	Greg's living in the house next door to us. He's only been in the U.S. for two weeks.	**Greg**	Oh, American football, of course. No, I've never played it, but I'd love to try. Are you on a team?
Greg	That's right. There's a lot to learn. Some things are really different here! I mean, what are those things?	**Emily**	OK, you two. That's enough about sports. Let's talk about something else!

(2) Correct the wrong information in each sentence.

1 Juan is waiting for Emily.   *No, Juan is waiting for Pete.*
2 Greg's dad is working in Brazil for a year. ....
3 Greg has been in the U.S. for a month. ....
4 Greg has seen lacrosse gloves before. ....
5 Juan is very good at lacrosse. ....
6 Juan thinks lacrosse is a little like field hockey. ....
7 Juan has never played American football. ....
8 Emily wants to talk more about sports. ....

Get talking Talking on the phone

3 Listen to the dialogues. Then read the texts and match them with the pictures.

1 **Girl** Hello, Steve. What are you doing?
   Boy Hi Sally. I'm doing my homework. And you?
   Girl I'm at the park.

2 **Boy** What are you doing, Monica?
   Girl I'm writing an email to my friend in California.

3 **Girl** Hello, Andy. What are you doing?
   Boy Hey, Joanna. I'm waiting for a bus. And you?
   Girl I'm buying new clothes for the party on Saturday.

4 Work with a partner. Make conversations similar to the ones in Exercise 3. Use the pictures below.

Language Focus

Vocabulary Sports apparel

  1 Match the words and pictures. Then listen and check.

☐ gloves
☐ sweatshirt
☐ helmet
☐ cleats
☐ pads
☐ tank top
☐ shorts
☐ socks
☐ goggles
☐ sneakers

2 Answer the questions about the sports apparel in Exercise 1.

1 For which things could we say "pair of ... ?"
2 Which things might people wear when they:
   a) go skateboarding?   c) ride bikes?   e) play tennis?
   b) play soccer?   d) go running?

> When people play ......, they wear cleats / shorts / knee pads / a helmet (etc.)

Get talking Buying things in a sporting goods store

 3 Number the dialogue in the correct order. Listen and check.

...... 10, I think.
..1.. May I help you?
...... Oh, they look fine. Can I try them on?
...... OK. What size do you wear?
...... Sure, no problem.
...... Well, we have these.
...... Yes. I need a pair of soccer cleats.

4 Work with a partner. Make similar conversations about:

- a football jersey
- a pair of sneakers
- a running top
- a pair of biking shorts

Grammar

Simple present / present continuous / present perfect (review)

1 **Look at the sentences and write the name of the correct tense: SP (simple present),**
PC (present continuous), or PP (present perfect).

1 **Do** you **play** football?   ....
2 **Have** you **heard** of lacrosse?   ....
3 He's **been** in the U.S. for two weeks.   ....
4 He's **living** in the house next door.   ....
5 I **don't play** very well.   ....
6 I'm not **talking** about soccer.   ....
7 I've never **played** it.   ....
8 We **live** in Kyoto.   ....
9 What **are** you **doing** here?   ....

2 **Match the questions and answers.**

1 Do you like tennis?
2 What are you doing?
3 Have you finished your homework?
4 What time do you go to school?
5 Do you like banana ice cream?
6 Has Sandra sent you an email?
7 Have you ever been to the U.S.?
8 What are you reading?

a) At eight o'clock.
b) Yes, but I'm not very good.
c) Yes, I'm opening it now.
d) No, but I want to go one day.
e) I'm writing an email to Johnny.
f) A book about Boston.
g) No. I'm still doing it.
h) I don't know. I've never had it.

3 **Circle the correct form of the verb.**

1 **A** Where's Pauline?
   B She's in her room. *She's talking / She talks* to her friend on the phone.
2 **A** Are you a good skater?
   B Yes, I am. *I go / I'm going* skating every weekend.
3 **A** Can I talk to you, please?
   B Not now, *I'm watching / I've watched* a TV show. Let's talk later.
4 **A** What's the matter?
   B I can't find my pen. *Have you seen / Are you seeing* it?
5 **A** She likes magazines.
   B Yes. *She reads / She's reading* every day.
6 **A** Is that a good book?
   B I don't know. *I don't read / I haven't read* it.

4 Match the sentences and the pictures.

1   Paula plays the guitar.
2   Paula's playing the guitar.
3   Alan's talking on the phone.
4   Alan talks on the phone a lot.

5   Our cat chases birds.
6   Our cat is chasing birds.
7   She sings really well.
8   She's singing really well right now.

5 Complete the sentences with the simple present or present continuous form of the verbs.

1   Sorry, I can't talk to you now. I'm having... dinner. (have)
2   In my house, we .... dinner at eight thirty. (have)
3   My father .... home to go to work at 7:30 every day. (leave)
4   Shhh! I .... television. (watch)
5   Do you know where Graham is? I .... for him. (look)
6   **A** I play tennis with Sally every Saturday.   **B** Really? Who ....? (win)
7   **A** The football game started 20 minutes ago.   **B** Oh? Who ....? (win)

6 Circle the correct verb.

1   Hey, here's the money! I *find / 've found* it!
2   We *live / have lived* in this house for 10 years.
3   Jane's sick, and she *doesn't go / hasn't been* to school for three days.
4   My parents are never here on Sunday afternoons. They *visit / have visited* my grandparents.
5   I don't know what happens in the movie because I *don't see / haven't seen* it.

7 Complete the sentences with the present perfect simple of the verb in parentheses.

1   Sorry, he isn't here. He's...gone... out. (go)
2   I .... never .... to go to Canada. (want)
3   I .... a new pair of sneakers. Do you like them? (buy)
4   .... you .... their new album? (hear)
5   Our teacher .... us a lot of homework for tonight. (give)
6   There are no apples left. You .... them all! (eat)
7   We're still waiting for the bus. It .... yet. (not come)
8   He's nervous because he .... for the exam. (not study)

Skills

Reading and speaking

1 **Read the texts. Match each text to a photo.**

A

B

C

Unusual American sports

1 Street luge

The luge is an Olympic event in which competitors ride a sled down an ice slide. Street luge is an extreme sport modeled on the luge. It takes place on a paved road and its competitors ride modified skateboards. Street luge began in southern California and the first professional race took place in 1975. This sport is dangerous, so there are many safety rules to help keep participants safe.

2 Catfish grabbing

Catfish grabbing is also known as catfish grappling, stumping, grabbling, noodling, or graveling. Basically, it is catching a catfish with your bare hands. Most of the time the catfish caught in this sport are released. But every now and again a catfish might end up being fried and eaten. Catfish grabbing is popular on the Tennessee River, but also takes place in the southern states.

3 Logrolling

Logrolling is also known as birling. It originated in the northwestern United States. In logrolling, two people stand on opposite sides of a log in a river or another body of water. One log roller starts moving the log by walking, while the other tries to stay balanced. The first person to fall off the log and into the water loses.

2 **Read these sentences. Which sport is each sentence about?**

1 It's a fairly dangerous sport.
2 You use your bare hands.
3 It started in southern California.
4 It is most common in the South.
5 The loser gets wet!

3 **Discuss in small groups.**

1 Do you consider these to be sports? Why/why not?
2 Which one would you like to take part in most? Why?
3 What unusual sports do you know of in your country?

Listening

4 Listen to an American boy talking about his trip to an Argentinian soccer game. Answer these questions.

1 Which country was Sam in?
2 Which team was playing?
3 Who won?

5 Listen again. Decide if the sentences below are T (True) or F (False).

1 The Boca Juniors play at La Bombonera.	T / F
2 The weather was warm.	T / F
3 The game started at 6:00 p.m.	T / F
4 Sam thought the stadium was quiet.	T / F
5 Sam sang along with the fans.	T / F
6 Sam thought the second half was boring.	T / F
7 Boca Juniors won the game 3–2.	T / F
8 Sam really enjoyed the evening.	T / F

Speaking

6 Choose a sentence for each photo. Compare your answers with a partner and explain your reasons.

1 Everyone had a great time.
2 We won!
3 It was really exciting.
4 The noise was incredible.

5 It was just for fun.
6 There were so many people there!
7 It was a really important game.
8 We lost but it didn't matter.

7 Tell your partner about a memorable sporting occasion.

Writing for your Portfolio

8 **Complete Roberto's text using the words on the left.**

country
wait
together
painted
unfortunately
interested
windows
sad

Three years ago it was the Soccer World Cup. I'm not really very ¹ .... in soccer, but my sister plays and really loves it. So we had a good time when we sat down ² .... and watched the games on TV, especially when our ³ .... played!

We were very excited when our country got to the semifinal. And people in our city went crazy, too! They put flags in the ⁴ .... of their houses, and people wore shirts with the team colors. On the day of the game, a lot of people ⁵ .... their faces, too. It was great!

We went to our neighbor's house to watch the semifinal. It started at eight o'clock at night. The game was pretty exciting, but ⁶ ...., we lost 2–1. We were all a little ⁷ ...., but it didn't matter very much because we all had a good time.

Now I can't ⁸ .... for the next Soccer World Cup. It's next year!

9 **Read the text again and answer the questions.**

1 Which sport is the story about?
2 What did people put in the windows of their houses?
3 What did people do to their faces?
4 Where did Roberto watch the semifinal?
5 Who won the match?
6 What is Roberto looking forward to?

10 **Write a text entitled "A sports event I remember."**

1 Was it a sporting event that you took part in or watched?
2 Where was the event? Or where did you watch it?
3 Who else was there?
4 What was the atmosphere like?
5 What were your expectations?
6 What happened?
7 How did you feel about it?
8 Why do you still remember this occasion?

Sounds right /s/ vs. /z/

11 **Listen to some of the words from Exercise 1, page 6. Decide which end with a /s/ sound and which end with a /z/ sound.**

/s/		/z/	

Early U.S. history

Key words

belief	harvest	turkey	tax
successful	native	colony	merchants
fight	corn	independent	harbor

1 Read the article about the Pilgrims. Match the questions and the paragraphs.

a) What happened when they got to America?
b) How do Americans remember them today?
c) Who were they?
d) Why did they travel to America?
e) How and when did they go to America?

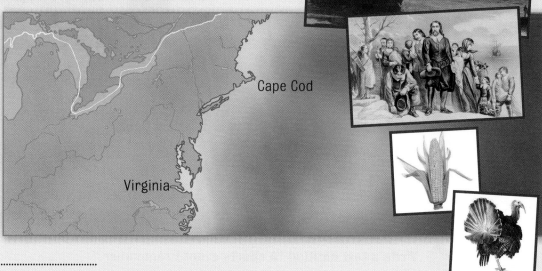

THE PILGRIMS

Cape Cod

Virginia

1 ....
The Pilgrims were Puritans. The Puritans were people who lived in England in the 16th and 17th centuries. Many people didn't like them because their beliefs were very different. A lot of Puritans went to live in Holland, but they weren't very happy there, either.

2 ....
People called America the "New World." They thought that America was a place where they could be rich and happy—a place where they could live as they wanted. So some Puritans decided to go to America.

3 ....
On August 5, 1620, a group of 101 Pilgrims went to America in a ship called *The Mayflower*. They left England and began a six-week journey to the New World. Many people died on the journey.

4 ....
The Pilgrims did not have enough food. But they were lucky because friendly Native Americans showed them how to hunt animals, make sugar, and grow corn. The Pilgrims also found a strange bird that they could eat—the turkey.

5 ....
In fall 1621, the Pilgrims had their first successful harvest. To say "thank you," they had a special meal with turkey. This was the first Thanksgiving. In 1863, Thanksgiving became a national holiday in the U.S. It is celebrated on the fourth Thursday in November every year. To this day, turkey is normally served for Thanksgiving dinner.

2 What do you know about the Boston Tea Party? Decide whether the statements below are T (True) or F (False).

The Boston Tea Party

1 In the 1700s, Boston was a small port. T / F
2 In 1770, North America was still a colony of Great Britain. T / F
3 Americans had to pay taxes to Great Britain. T / F
4 Americans went on to a ship in Boston Harbor and threw boxes of tea into the ocean. T / F
5 The tea on the ships belonged to the British government. T / F
6 After the Boston Tea Party, the British government closed Boston Harbor. T / F

3 Helen, a student, is giving a presentation to her class about the Boston Tea Party. Listen and check your answers.

Mini-project A moment in time

Write a project about an important event in your country's history.

Look for information on the Internet or in a library. Write a text that includes:
• A description of what happened.
• Why it is considered so important now.
Use pictures to illustrate the text and present the information in a poster to your class.

UNIT ② Space and beyond

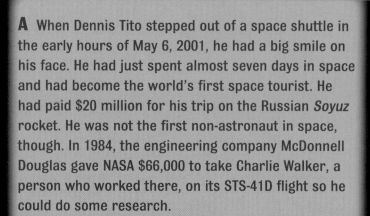

① **Read the texts.**

In this unit

You learn
- past continuous vs. simple past
- past perfect
- narrative tenses (review)
- words for travel

and then you can
- give reasons
- talk about your trip to school

A When Dennis Tito stepped out of a space shuttle in the early hours of May 6, 2001, he had a big smile on his face. He had just spent almost seven days in space and had become the world's first space tourist. He had paid $20 million for his trip on the Russian *Soyuz* rocket. He was not the first non-astronaut in space, though. In 1984, the engineering company McDonnell Douglas gave NASA $66,000 to take Charlie Walker, a person who worked there, on its STS-41D flight so he could do some research.

B A space shuttle takes 90 minutes to orbit Earth. In these 90 minutes, daylight and nighttime change for the astronauts. Altogether, 45 minutes of the journey are spent in daylight, and 45 minutes are in the dark. In fact, during a 24-hour period they see 16 sunsets and 16 sunrises!

C Astronauts on the shuttle can choose from about 100 different food items and 50 drinks. However, a word of warning: The taste of food often changes in space and your favorite food on the ground might taste disgusting 200 kilometers above Earth.

D The first people to travel into space were Russian. The first people to go to the moon were American. When Neil Armstrong took his first steps on the moon, millions were watching him on TV back home. Of course, everyone knows Armstrong was the first man on the moon. But did you know that his Apollo 11 mission left a plaque on the moon? It says, "Here men from the planet Earth first set foot upon the Moon July 1969, A.D. We came in peace for all mankind."

E Space travel has always been a dangerous business. Two of the most tragic accidents in the last 30 years were the *Challenger* and *Columbia* space shuttle disasters. In 1986, the *Challenger* had only been in the sky for a minute when it exploded. In 2003, the *Columbia* broke up while it was reentering Earth's atmosphere. On both flights all seven members of the crew died.

2 Match the titles with the correct paragraph from the text. There is one additional title.

1 A "day" in space? ☐
2 When things go wrong ☐
3 Eating in space ☐
4 A message on the moon ☐
5 Paying passengers ☐
6 Who owns space? ☐

Get talking Giving reasons

3 Listen and repeat.

A Why was Dave so angry?
B Because someone had stolen his wallet.

A Why was Shenna so tired?
B Because she hadn't slept all night.

4 Work with a partner. Look at the pictures and say the moods.

sad   nervous   excited   happy   hungry   bored

A A is sad.

B B is …

5 Work with a partner. Choose a prompt from below and act out dialogues like the ones in Exercise 3.

A Why was George sad?
B Because his friend had forgotten his birthday.

• watch TV all day
• not study for exam
• friend forget birthday
• get ticket for favorite band
• pass driving test
• not eat all day

Language Focus

Vocabulary Travel

1 **Match the sentences and pictures.**

Minnie is a pilot. Every day she flies from Chicago O'Hare to Washington, D.C., and back.

  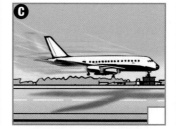 

1 Minnie sets out for work around 5:30 a.m.
2 She gets into her car.
3 She gets to the airport around 6:10 a.m.
4 She gets on the plane at 6:50 a.m., half an hour before the passengers.
5 The plane takes off at 7:30 a.m.
6 The trip takes around an hour and a half. The plane lands around 9:00 a.m.
7 After a rest in Washington, D.C., she flies back. She gets off the plane around 4:00 p.m.
8 She drives home. She gets out of her car around 5:00 p.m.

Get talking Talking about your trip to school

 11

2 **Write the phrases on the right under the questions. Then listen and check.**

A How do you get to school?
B ¹ ....
A What time do you set out?
B ² ....

A What time do you get to school?
B ³ ....
A How long does the trip take?
B ⁴ ....

> I leave the house at 20 past eight.
>
> I arrive around ten to nine.
>
> Half an hour.
>
> On foot usually, but my mom drives me if I'm late.

3 **Practice the dialogues with a partner. Then find out how your partner gets to school.**

Grammar

Past continuous vs. simple past

1 **Look at the example and circle the two actions. Which action is shorter?**

In 2003, the *Columbia* broke up while it was reentering Earth's atmosphere.

2 **Look at the pictures and write sentences.**

1 Steve race down the hill / he fall off.

....

2 Jeff cook / a bird fly into the window.

....

3 Oliver fish / he see a crocodile.

....

4 Susan walk on the beach / a wave hit her

....

5 Julia run to school / the clock strike nine

....

6 Lana stand at the bus stop / a car soak her with water

....

Past perfect

3 **Look at the examples and answer the questions.**

A When Dennis Tito had a smile on his face, he had just spent almost seven days in space.

B In 1986, the *Challenger* had only been in the sky for a minute when it exploded.

1 In sentence A, why did Tito have a smile on his face?
2 In sentence B, did the *Challenger* explode as it took off or after it had taken off?

Rule
We use the past perfect to emphasize that one action in the past happened before another.

4 **Circle the verb that is in the past perfect tense.**

1 I hadn't finished my homework, but I still went to bed.
2 After she had done the dishes, she read her book.
3 When James arrived home, he found someone had taken his TV.
4 I didn't buy the coat because I hadn't brought enough money with me.
5 When I got to school, I realized I had left my books at home.

5 Complete the sentences using the past perfect and simple past tense.

1 When I .... her face, I knew I .... her before. (see/meet)
2 He .... two pizzas because he .... all day. (order/not eat)
3 I ...., so I .... the exam really difficult. (not study/find)
4 Anna .... home because she .... all her money. (go/spend)

Narrative tenses (review)

6 Look at the sentences from the text on page 14 and answer the questions.

A He had paid $20 million for his trip.
B McDonnell Douglas gave NASA $66,000 to take Charlie Walker on its flight.
C When Dennis Tito stepped out of a space shuttle, he had a big smile on his face.
D Did you know that his Apollo 11 mission left a plaque on the moon?
E When Neil Armstrong took his first steps on the moon, millions were watching him on TV.

Which sentences contain an example of:

1 the simple past with a regular verb?   *Sentence C* ....
2 the simple past with an irregular verb? ....
3 a simple past question? ....
4 the past continuous? ....
5 the past perfect? ....

7 Complete the short story using words from the box.

| got | were walking | had left | didn't take |
| took | had just got in | was shining | were moving |

It was a beautiful morning. The sun ¹............. and there was a cool breeze in the air. It was the perfect day for a picnic. Everyone ²............. into the car. We kids were really excited. A day at the beach and a picnic sounded like the perfect day. The journey there ³............. long, and we were soon there. We ⁴............. everything out of the car and started to go down to the beach. While we ⁵............., we saw dark clouds over the ocean. They ⁶............. quickly toward us. We ran back to the car, just in time. We ⁷............. when the rain started. Oh well, we still had the picnic. A picnic in the car could be fun. Then Mom opened the picnic basket. I looked at her face and knew immediately. She ⁸............. the picnic at home!

8 Look at the pictures. Choose one to create a story with a partner. Then tell the story to the class. Use the sentences below to start.

As they set out into the jungle, they did not know what was waiting for them ...

As the plane took off, I realized I'd dropped my wallet somewhere ...

Skills

Listening

 1 **Listen to the radio advertisement and complete the text.**

THE RACE FOR SPACE

Human history is full of stories of explorers who have risked their lives to go places no one has ever been before, from the top of the highest mountain to the bottom of the deepest ocean. Would you like to join them? You can win $1.................... million at the same time!

We are offering the Ansari X prize to the first people to build a spaceship that can be used more than once. Interested? These are the rules:

1 The spaceship must be able to carry 2................. adults.

2 The spaceship must reach a height of 3............... This height is where a space orbit begins.

3 The spaceship must return with no 4.................. and no injury to any of the crew.

4 A second flight must be made within 5................. weeks using the same spacecraft.

5 No government 6.................. can be used in the project.

Does that sound easy? What are you waiting for?

  2 **Listen to the radio news and put a check (✓) next to the correct options.**

1 Which spacecraft won the Ansari X prize?

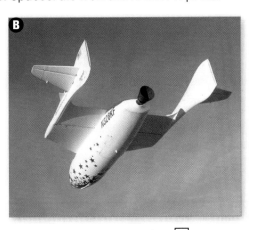
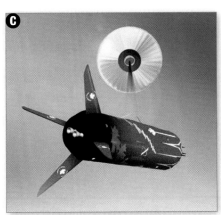

a) *Canadian Arrow* ☐

b) *SpaceShipOne* ☐

c) *da Vinci Wild Fire* ☐

2 How high did the spacecraft fly?
a) 100km ☐   b) 110km ☐   c) 115km ☐

3 When did the flight take place?
a) 10/4/2004 ☐   b) 11/4/2004 ☐   c) 10/14/2004 ☐

4 Who flew the plane?
a) Peter Diamandis ☐   b) Paul Allen ☐   c) Brian Binnie ☐

5 Which company wants to use *SpaceShipOne* for commercial flights?
a) Virgin Atlantic ☐   b) Virgin Space ☐   c) Virgin Galactic ☐

6 How much will a flight into space cost?
a) $20,000 ☐   b) $200,000 ☐   c) $2,000,000 ☐

7 How many people does Richard Branson want to put into space during the next five years?
a) 3,000 ☐   b) 13,000 ☐   c) 30,000 ☐

Listening

  3 **Listen to the poem and complete each sentence with the correct word.**

Journey to Mars

I wish I could go back in [1].......................
To a place that I called mine.
Twenty years ago you would find
Life was simple and people were [2].......................

But now the streets echo to the [3].......................
Of so much trouble all around.
Of people mean and [4].......................
Children neglected and needy.

I'm going to Mars
up among the [5].......................
I'm leaving this town.
Letting everyone down.
I'm leaving my [6]....................... behind.
Out of sight and out of mind.

With a [7]....................... and tired face
I travel up into space.
No money for a round-trip flight
On my own, I hope I'm [8].......................
A journey into the unknown.
A new world, a new home.

4 **Read the poem and decide if the statements are T (True) or F (False).**

1 The man is happy because he is going to the moon. T / F
2 He is leaving his family behind. T / F
3 The rocket leaves in a few minutes. T / F
4 He plans to come back soon. T / F

Speaking and writing

5 **Discuss the questions with a partner. Then write a story about the poem.**

l Who is this man? (Name, age, profession, etc).
2 Who is he leaving behind? Why can't they go with him?
3 Why does he have to leave?
4 Where is he going, and why can't he come back?
5 What is going to happen when he arrives in his new world?

6 **Read aloud your stories about the man in the poem.**

Check your progress Units 1 and 2

1 Complete the names of the objects.

1 football cl _ _ _ _ 　　4 swimming go _ _ _ _ _ _
2 a pair of glo _ _ _ 　　5 a pair of sne _ _ _ _ _
3 biking hel _ _ _ 　　　6 knee p _ _ _

☐ 6

2 Complete the sentences.

1 He sets _ _ _ for work at 7:00 a.m.
2 I go to school _ _ foot. It's not too far.
3 We need to get to the a _ _ _ _ _ _ now to catch the plane.
4 When I get _ _ a plane, I'm always nervous.
5 Our plane takes _ _ _ at 9:00 a.m.
6 Did you have a good tr _ _ here?
7 The plane I _ _ _ _ at 11:00 a.m., and we'll take the bus after that.
8 How does your mom _ _ _ to work?

☐ 8

3 Complete the dialogues.

Sam What ¹............... you doing?
Dave ²............... surfing the Internet. And you?
Sam Not much. I'm really bored.
Dave Why are you so bored?
Sam ³............... I can't think of anything to do.
Dave Why don't you come over? We can do something together.
Sam Great! See you in half an hour.

Salesclerk ⁴............... I help you?
Harry Yes, I need a blue football jersey.
Salesclerk What ⁵............... would you like?
Harry This one looks good. Can I ⁶............... it on, please?
Salesclerk Sure. Go ahead.

☐ 6

4 Write the questions.

1 ....
　 Yes, I love tennis!
2 ....
　 Emily's training to become an astronaut.
3 ....
　 John broke his dad's clock.

☐ 6

5 Complete the sentences with the correct form of the present continuous.

1 Sam and Dave .... (talk) on the phone.
2 I .... (try) to help you!
3 You .... (not / listen) to me!
4 .... (we / leave) now?
5 We should be quiet. My brothers .... (study)!
6 .... (she / shop) for clothes?

☐ 12

6 Circle the correct tense.

1 I *had finished / have finished* all my homework when he called.
2 *Have you ever played / Are you ever playing* football for your school team?
3 I *don't like / am not liking* many sports, but I *am loving / love* swimming.
4 She *is sleeping / sleeps,* so don't wake her up.
5 What *are you doing / do you do* on Saturdays?

☐ 6

7 Write the missing words.

Last week I went to a football game at school. It was a great game and I ¹......... enjoying the action. But then a player was hurt and had to go off. It was bad news for my team because we ²......... losing 2–0 and there ³......... only half an hour left to play.

Then, the coach came up to me and asked me if I could play! Luckily, I ⁴......... brought my uniform with me. So I quickly changed, pulled my cleats on, and ran onto the field. I ⁵......... never scored for my team so I don't know why the coach chose me, but I did my best. You're not going to believe this, but I scored a touchdown! We ⁶......... the game and the coach said it was all thanks to me!

☐ 6

TOTAL ☐ 50

My progress so far is ...
😊 great! ☐   😐 good. ☐   ☹ poor. ☐

Trains, planes, and automobiles!

15 ① **Read the facts and circle T (True) or F (False). Listen and check your answers.**

1 From 1836 to 1926, a man had to walk in front of cars to warn people that they were coming. T/F
2 In 1962, John Glenn became the first American to circle Earth in the *Friendship 7*. T/F
3 A building where they build airships is so tall that clouds form and it rains inside. T/F
4 The woman pilot Amelia Earhart set three world records for flying in 1932. T/F
5 In 1939, the *Graf Zeppelin* airship flew nonstop around the world. T/F

② **Read and complete the text using the numbers in the box below. Compare your answers with a partner.**

23	1901	1999	three	20 million	2,200

Unusual solutions to transportation problems—past and present

From tuk-tuks to sky trains in Thailand
Tuk-tuks are ¹............-wheeled vehicles with a place for the driver in the front. People use them for short journeys in big cities in Thailand. Tuk-tuk engines make a funny sound (that's how this vehicle gets its name).
The fastest and cleanest way to travel around Bangkok is by SkyTrain. The first SkyTrain was built in ²............ to solve traffic problems in the city. It originally had ³............ stations, but they are building more all the time.

The view from the sky in Germany
It looks very modern, but the monorail in Wuppertal, Germany opened more than 100 years ago, in ⁴............, and it's the oldest working monorail in the world. The trains run on electricity, and they never stop due to bad weather. Of course, being 10 meters above the streets, they never get stuck in traffic either! The monorail carries more than ⁵............ passengers a year.

The sedan chair
This is basically just a covered seat on two long pieces of wood. One person at the front and another at the back carry the chair and its passenger. We don't know the exact history of the sedan chair, but we know they existed in the Han Dynasty in China about ⁶............ years ago.

③ **Now answer the questions.**

1 How did the tuk-tuk get its name?
2 How old is the German monorail?
3 In your opinion, which is the best way to travel?
4 List the advantages and disadvantages of each.

④  **World cities are becoming more congested and polluted. Work in groups. Design a new eco-friendly form of transportation.**

American MORE! Now you can watch Episode 1 of *School Reporters*!

Learn MORE about Culture

Emily was a quiet kid. She didn't say much, even to her mother. Her father was always too busy to listen anyway. She never caused any problems. Her grades at school were good. She got along with everyone, so her mother never worried, until the space paintings.

Emily had always loved to paint and she was good at it, too—very good. She spent all her pocket money on paint and paper. She'd started painting when she was seven. At first it had always been animals, flowers, and other things that she saw out of her bedroom window. As she got older, her subjects changed: cars, then people, and then sports events. Nothing strange there.

But then one day Emily found something new to paint. Scenes from outer space. But these weren't pictures of Mars or Saturn and its rings. These were paintings of weird and wonderful futuristic worlds. They showed planets with three suns. And there were strange forests where strange animals lived. Emily's mother had seen the paintings and wondered where her daughter got such far out ideas.

Emily's mother wanted to tell her husband about the paintings, but she didn't. Emily's father was a writer. A few years before, he had written a very successful science fiction series for TV. He was famous and got a lot of work. But now people were starting to forget about him, because he hadn't come up with anything good for a long time. So he had become depressed. He didn't want to talk to anyone, and he often got angry very quickly if someone disturbed him.

Emily was in her room. She had run out of paint, but she had no money left. She couldn't disturb her dad. He was in his office and no one was allowed to go in there—not even Emily's mother. Emily didn't want to wait, so she picked up some of her paintings and set out for the art store. She explained to the owner that she needed some paint but she didn't have any money. She asked the man if he wanted to buy some of her space scenes. He gave her $50 for four of them.

A few days later, Emily's dad was walking past the art store when he stopped and looked in the window. He saw the four paintings that Emily had done. He was fascinated by them. He walked into the store and bought them.

Emily's dad took the paintings home and put them on the wall in his office. He sat down in his chair, looked at the paintings, and started to write. For the next week, no one saw Emily's dad. Day after day, night after night, he locked himself in his office. All they heard was the sound of him working on his computer.

Then one day he came out of the office. Emily and her mother had never seen him so happy. "It's finished," he told them. "My masterpiece."

A week later they were celebrating. The TV studio loved his ideas for his new series and they were going to start filming it as soon as possible. A famous Hollywood actor was going to be in it. The series was simply called "Far Out."

For MORE! Go to www.cambridge.org/elt/americanmore and take a quiz on this text.

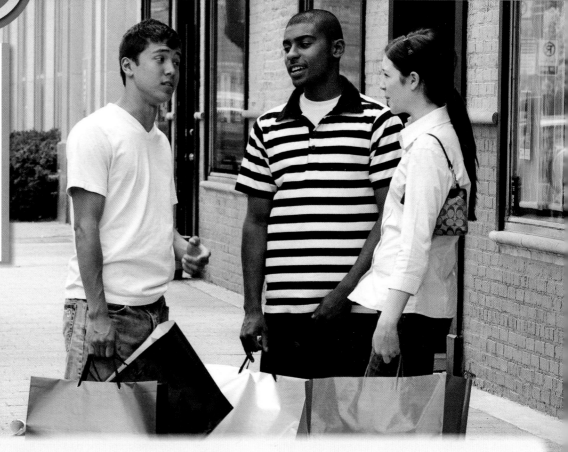

In this unit

You learn
- *should(n't)/ought*
- gerunds
- words for money and shopping

and then you can
- say what people ought to do
- talk about shopping

16

1 **Listen and read.**

Greg Boy, I'm exhausted! Shopping at the mall is really tiring!

Emily I know. That's why I like shopping online.

Greg Really? You shouldn't do a lot of online shopping, you know. It can be a little dangerous.

Emily I don't think so. Well, I've never had a problem anyway. And buying things online is so easy!

Greg That's true, but I can't shop online anyway.

Emily Why not?

Greg I don't have a debit card.

Emily You should have a debit card. They're useful.

Greg Yes, I know. I am getting one, but it hasn't arrived yet. Actually, it's taking a long time. We asked the bank for it two weeks ago.

Emily You probably ought to find out what's happening.

Greg Yeah, you're right.

Emily Look, there's Juan! Hi, Juan!

Juan Hi, you two. Listen, there's a great new bookstore on 32nd Street. You should go and look around. It has a great secondhand section.

Emily Secondhand? No way! I don't want to buy things that someone else has used.

Juan Oh, come on, Emily. They're books, not clothes!

Emily Well, maybe I'll go, but not now. I ought to go home.

Greg OK, see you, Emily! Now, Juan, where's this bookstore?

2 Check (✓) the correct answer.

1 Emily likes

a) shopping online. ☐   b) buying secondhand clothes. ☐
c) shopping at the mall. ☐

2 Greg can't

a) spend a lot of money. ☐   b) pay in cash. ☐   c) shop online. ☐

3 Emily thinks that Greg should

a) find a credit card. ☐   b) talk to his mother. ☐
c) talk to the bank about his debit card. ☐

4 Juan has found

a) a good bookstore. ☐   b) a good clothing store. ☐   c) an old bookstore. ☐

5 Emily is going

a) to buy secondhand clothes. ☐   b) to the bookstore. ☐   c) home. ☐

Get talking Saying what people ought to do

17 **3** Listen and repeat.

A I don't feel well.
B You ought to go to the doctor.

A I hate grocery shopping.
B You ought to shop online.

A I don't have enough money for a new bike.
B You ought to buy a secondhand one.

4 Work with a partner. Make similar dialogues. Use an idea from column A and an idea from column B.

A	B
I need some exercise.	… go to your room and study.
I'm really tired.	… read a book.
I have a test tomorrow.	… go swimming.
I don't know what to do this afternoon.	… go for a walk.
I'm bored.	… watch a movie on DVD.
There's nothing good on television.	… take a nap.

Language Focus

Vocabulary Money and shopping

1 Read the texts. Who do you think is speaking? Match each text with a picture.

A

B **C**

We have to be careful with money at the moment. We're going to need a lot of new things when the baby arrives, so we are trying to *save* our money. I don't mind not buying things. It's still fun *window shopping*. When we do buy things, we always pay by *debit card*. ☐

───

You have to be careful with money when you're a student. When you've bought all your books, paid the rent, and bought some clothes, there's not a lot left. You have to be careful not to *waste* it on things. I usually buy a lot of *secondhand* things. It's cheaper. I always pay in *cash*. ☐

───

Money? Money's no problem. I make loads of it and *spend* a lot of it, too. I often go on a *spending spree*. I always buy the best—*brand new* things. TVs, computers, cars. I always pay by *credit card*—buy now, pay later! ☐

2 Find the words in italics in the text and write them in the table below.

Things you can do with money:	Ways of paying for something:	Shopping activities:
1............ You can 2............ it 3............	You can pay by 4............ in 5............ by 6............	do some 7............ .... go on a 8............ ....
Adjectives to describe things you buy:		
9... 10...		

Get talking Talking about shopping

18 **3** Complete the dialogues. Listen and check.

> Only $1.50   A lot of clothes!   Just some secondhand books.
> I have been on a spending spree!   In cash.

1 A What did you buy?
   B 1.................................
   A How much were they?
   B 2.................................
   A How did you pay?
   B 3.................................

2 A Where've you been?
   B 4.................................
   A What did you buy?
   B 5.................................

4 Work with a partner. Practice the dialogues.

Grammar

Should(n't) / ought

1 **Who says these sentences in the dialogue on page 24? Match the sentences and people.**

1 You shouldn't do a lot of online shopping.
2 You should have a debit card.
3 You should go and look around.
4 I ought to go home.

a) Emily to Greg.
b) Emily to Juan and Greg.
c) Juan to Emily and Greg.
d) Greg to Emily.

2 **Complete the rule with *should* / *ought to* / *infinitive*.**

We can use [1]............... / *shouldn't* to say what we think is a good idea, and to give advice, They are followed by the [2]............... of the verb.

We can also use [3]............... + the infinitive of the verb. We don't use *ought* as often as we use *should*.

3 **Match the sentences and responses.**

1 My room's a mess.
2 I'm not feeling very well.
3 I think we've upset Joanna.
4 It's raining hard now.
5 I get really bad grades at school.
6 Bob's had another accident.

a) Perhaps you should study more.
b) You should clean it up.
c) I don't think we should go out.
d) You ought to see a doctor.
e) He shouldn't drive so fast.
f) Yes, we should say "sorry."

4 **Complete the sentences using the phrases below.**

should go	shouldn't go	should do	ought to buy
should ask	should ask	ought to learn	ought to tell

1 **A** We're lost! **B** You're right. I think we .... someone for directions.
2 **A** I've lost John's pen. **B** Well, I think you .... him.
3 **A** How can I get better grades? **B** I think you .... your homework.
4 **A** I feel terrible. **B** Perhaps you .... to the doctor.
5 **A** Our TV is really old. **B** You're right. Dad .... a new one.
6 **A** I'm going to Peru on vacation. **B** Great! You .... some Spanish before you go.
7 **A** The teacher gets mad at me sometimes. **B** I don't think you .... so many questions.
8 **A** The sign says "Do not disturb." **B** You .... in.

Gerunds

5 Read the sentences from the dialogue on page 24. Circle the correct verbs.

1 *Shop / Shopping* at the mall is really tiring!

2 *Buy / Buying* things online is so easy!

6 Complete the rule with *subject* and *–ing*.

The Gerund (the ¹............ form of a verb) can be used as the ²............ or as the object of a verb.

7 Complete the sentences using the verbs below.

watching	doing	playing	eating	going	staying	taking

1 I don't like .... in expensive restaurants.
2 .... online games is really boring!
3 .... tests is the hardest thing for me.
4 I love .... in nice hotels when we are on vacation.
5 .... the dishes is the worst job in the world!
6 .... out to the movie theater is OK, but I prefer .... movies on TV.

8 Complete the sentences with the gerund of the verb in parentheses.

1 .... old movies on TV is a lot of fun. (watch)
2 I really don't like .... very much. (dance)
3 .... clothes is my brother's favorite thing. (buy)
4 .... my dog for a walk is good exercise. (take)
5 I hate .... late for school. (be)

9 Complete each sentence using the idea in the picture.

1 Brad really enjoys .listening. to music.

2 .... takes a lot of practice.

3 .... with my friends is my favorite thing.

4 My father loves ....

5 .... is the best thing to do on winter mornings.

6 Jennifer can't stand .... in the rain.

Skills

Reading and speaking

1 Read the quiz and fill in the blanks using the words below. Then take the quiz.

bought	buy	shopping	save	window	by	cash

Is your shopping out of control?

1 Your grandmother gives you $50 for your birthday. Do you:
[A] go straight to the mall?
[B] buy a DVD and .... the rest?
[C] put it all in the bank?

2 Monday is a holiday and you have the day off school. Do you:
[A] go to the mall with your friends?
[B] go out for the day with your family?
[C] stay in and do your English assignment?

3 Do you usually pay for something:
[A] .... borrowing money?
[B] by debit card?
[C] in ....?

4 When was the last time you .... something?
[A] today
[B] last week
[C] last month

5 What do you spend most of your time on the computer doing?
[A] online ....
[B] playing games
[C] chatting with friends

6 You walk past your favorite store. It's closed. Do you:
[A] spend 10 minutes doing some ....
shopping?
[B] have a quick look in the window and then walk away?
[C] walk straight past?

7 You need a new computer. Do you:
[A] .... a brand new one?
[B] look in the newspaper for a secondhand one?
[C] see if any of your friends happen to have a spare one?

2 Discuss the questions and your answers with a partner.

3 Look at the key. Add up your score and find out what kind of shopper you are. Do you agree?

> **Key:**
> A answers = 2 points
> B answers = 1 point
> C answers = 0 points

10–14 points: You live for the weekend and the chance to get to the mall. And when stores aren't open, you're probably online buying things. Do you think it would be a good idea to find another hobby?

5–9 points: You enjoy a good day's shopping every now and then, but it's not the most important thing in your life. Your shopping is under control.

0–4 points: You really don't enjoy shopping at all, do you? There's just one question; if you don't like shopping, how do you ever get new things? Perhaps it's time you learned to overcome your fear.

Reading and listening

(4) **Read the text and find out what the rule of Buy Nothing Day is.**

What is Buy Nothing Day? It's a day where you challenge yourself, your family, and your friends to stop shopping and enjoy life. Anyone can take part. All you need to do is spend a day without spending!

The message is simple—shop less and live more! The challenge is to try simple living for a day and spend time with family and friends, rather than spend money on them.

Of course, Buy Nothing Day isn't about changing your lifestyle for just one day. We want it to be something you think about every day. We want people to make a commitment to buying less, recycling more, and challenging companies to clean up and be fair.

To celebrate this year we are holding swap stores where you can exchange your things with other people, free concerts and shows, and, best of all, a cut-up-your-credit-card table. Remember, there is only one rule for this day—BUY NOTHING!

19 **(5)** **Listen to Mark Goodwill talking about Buy Nothing Day and circle the correct answer.**

1 Buy Nothing Day is:
   A less than five years old.
   B less than 10 years old.
   C more than 10 years old.

2 Buy Nothing Day is celebrated:
   A in Korea only.
   B in Europe only.
   C all over the world.

3 The organizers think that shopping is:
   A bad for the environment.
   B a waste of money.
   C bad for our health.

4 A shopping-free zone is an area:
   A where you don't pay for anything.
   B where shopping is banned.
   C where people do things to get shoppers' attention.

5 To organize a "choo-choo" you need
   A 13 people.
   B 15 people.
   C 20 people.

6 One thing you should do is:
   A give out leaflets.
   B annoy people who are shopping.
   C have fun.

Reading

6 **Read the extracts from the emails and answer the questions.**

1 How much allowance does Sam get?
2 How much was the DVD that Ollie bought?
3 How old is Donna's dad?
4 What is the name of the person in the picture?

...I bought a DVD on Saturday. I gave the salesclerk $10, and he gave me change. However, when I got home I checked my change and I realized that he'd given me change for $50. That means I got the DVD and I'm $42 richer. I can get the money to get a new game and still have some left. The thing is, though, I feel bad about keeping it. It's a lot of money and the salesclerk might get in trouble. But $42 is a lot of money. It could make me very happy... (Ollie)

...It's my dad's birthday on Sunday, and I want to get him a really special present—something to say "thanks" for the help he's given me with my exams. Plus it's his last year in his forties! The only problem is, I don't know what to get him. He loves fishing and especially old books about fishing, but I have no idea where I could find them. So I'm trying to think of something else, but I just don't know what to get him. He's so difficult to buy for. I don't suppose you have any ideas. I mean, what would you buy your dad?... (Donna)

... I was in Top Girl on Saturday. You'll never guess what, but they have some really cool leather boots. They're beautiful. I was going to buy them and then I looked at the price: $99.99. That's almost $100. I don't have that kind of money. I only have $50. It would take me another two months' allowance to save up enough (and that's if I don't spend a penny on anything else). But I want them so bad. They'd be perfect for Molly's birthday next month. Oh, what am I going to do? ... (Sam)

Speaking and writing

7 **Work in small groups. Discuss what you think Sam, Ollie, and Donna should do.**

8 **Choose one of the emails and write a reply saying what you think the person should do.**

Sounds right Spelling

9 **Practice spelling aloud the names of the people who wrote the emails in Exercise 6. Then think of five people in your class and spell their names to your partner, who writes them down. Then switch roles.**

Space travel

Key words

jet of water	mass	force	reaction engine
orbit	orbiter	accelerate	rocket booster
hose	launch	thrust	mph (miles per hour)

 Read the text and write three questions to ask your partner.

How things work: Rocket engines

How do rockets work? Here are a few of the problems that space engineers have to solve when they build rockets:

- What kind of engine can get a rocket into space?
- How will the rocket cope with extreme temperatures? Metal gets very hot at high speeds.
- How can they get the rocket back into Earth's atmosphere?

The engine

Car engines use the principle of rotation to turn the wheels. Rockets don't have wheels, so a different kind of engine is needed—an engine that can "throw" the rocket (a huge and heavy piece of metal) hundreds of kilometers into the sky.

What a rocket needs is a reaction engine. Reaction engines work on a famous scientific principle discovered by Sir Isaac Newton. The principle says: "For every action, there is an equal and opposite reaction."

Let's look at this principle in a simple way. Have you ever seen firefighters dealing with a fire using a big water hose? These hoses throw out a weight of water that produces a force in the opposite direction. This force can be very strong and this is why there are usually two firefighters holding the hose. If the jet of water was too strong for the firefighters, they would go flying back in the opposite direction.

A rocket engine throws mass in the form of a high-pressure gas. The engine throws the mass of gas out in one direction in order to get a reaction in the opposite direction. The mass comes from the weight of the fuel that the rocket engine burns. The burning process accelerates the mass of fuel so that it comes out of the rocket at high speed.

If you have ever seen a space shuttle launch, you will know that there are three parts:

- the orbiter
- the big external tank
- the two solid rocket boosters (SRBs)

The orbiter weighs around 75,000 kilograms when it's empty. The external tank weighs 35,000 kilograms empty. The two solid rocket boosters weigh 84,000 kilograms each when they are empty. But you have to load in the fuel. Each SRB holds 500,000 kilograms of fuel. The external tank holds 541,000 liters of liquid oxygen (616,000 kilograms) and 1.5 million liters of liquid hydrogen (103,000 kilograms). The whole vehicle—shuttle, external tank, solid rocket boosters, and all the fuel—has a total weight of 2 million kilograms at launch. That's 2 million kilograms to push 75,000 kilograms into orbit!

All that fuel is being thrown out the back of the space shuttle at a speed of 10,000 kilometers per hour. The SRBs burn for about two minutes and generate about 1.5 million kilograms of thrust each at launch. The three main engines burn for about eight minutes, generating 170,000 kilograms of thrust each during the burn.

Mini-project Finding out about space

Choose one of the following questions. Go to a library or use the Internet to find out more about it. Write a short text. Add images if you can.

- One of the challenges with space travel is how to get a spacecraft safely back to Earth. Why is this so? How can scientists make sure that a rocket doesn't burn up under the high temperatures?

- The United States and Russia have had orbiting space stations since 1971 and are now cooperating with other nations to build the International Space Station, a place that will make it possible for humans to stay in space permanently. What will the space station look like? What will it be like to live and work in space? What problems are involved in establishing a space station? What will it be used for?

- Apophis, a 45-million-ton rock, a so-called asteroid, is orbiting the sun at 28,000 mph. If it hits Earth, it could easily destroy a large city. In 2029, it'll be closer to us than our moon is. Find out more about asteroids. What are they? What does modern science say could be done to avoid an asteroid's collision with planet Earth?

UNIT ④ A working life

1 Listen and read.

In this unit

You learn
- *be going to* / present continuous (review)
- future time clauses
- adjectives for personality

and then you can
- say what you want to do
- talk about personalities and jobs

Mandy

Philip

What do you want to do when you graduate?

I want to be a soldier. So as soon as I graduate, I'll join the army. My mom isn't very happy about that. But I'd love to be part of a U.N. peacekeeping force. There are a lot of people in the world who need protection. I'd like to help them.

I'm going to be a dancer. I know it might seem unusual and a couple of my friends make jokes about it. But it's what I love and there's nothing I like more. My mom and dad are cool about it. They know I'm good at dancing and they know I'm hardworking, too.

Are you doing anything now to help you get where you want to be?

You have to be in top shape to get into the army, so I work out a lot. And in about six months, I'm having my first interview to join the army, so I'm getting ready for that.

Yes, of course. I'm always dancing. I have ballet and tap lessons every week, and next summer, I'm taking lessons in Flamenco dancing. After I finish that, I'll be an even better dancer.

What jobs would you never want to do?

I could never do anything that involves working with children. I could never be a teacher, for example. I'm not patient enough. I'd hate to teach someone like me, for example!

I don't think I could be a doctor or a dentist. I don't like the sight of blood. It's funny because my dad's a dentist and my mom's a nurse.

What's more important, money or enjoying what you do?

Money is important. I mean, you can't live without it. But I don't need a lot of money to be happy. I think it's more important to enjoy what you do. No matter what I do, I'm going to enjoy every minute.

Both are important. Most dancers don't get paid much money, but I'm going to make a lot of money, I think, because I know I'm going to be successful. Am I arrogant? Maybe. Ambitious? Absolutely!

2 Write *Mandy* or *Philip* in each space.

1 .... wants to be a soldier.
2 ....'s parents think he/she is making a good choice.
3 .... wants to help people.
4 .... wants to do something he/she is very good at.
5 ....'s parents work in health care.
6 .... wouldn't like to work with children.
7 .... wants to make a lot of money.
8 .... doesn't care a lot about money.

Get talking Saying what you want to do

3 Match the questions with possible answers. There are two answers for each question. Then listen and check.

1 What are you going to become when you graduate?
2 Why did you choose that?
3 What job would you never want to do?
4 Why?

a) I'd hate to be a farmer.
b) I want to be a police officer.
c) Because I love animals.
d) I could never be a writer.
e) Because I don't like working alone.
f) I'm not sure yet, but maybe a vet.
g) Because I like helping people.
h) Because I don't like getting out of bed early.

4 Work with a partner. Ask them the questions from Exercise 3. Then switch roles.

A What are you going to become when you graduate?

B I'm not sure yet. Maybe I'll be a teacher.

Language Focus

Vocabulary Personality adjectives

22 **1** Complete the sentences with the correct word. Use the people's names to help you. Then listen and check.

ambitious
hardworking
creative
helpful
easygoing
patient
~~friendly~~
polite

 1 Freda is _friendly_

 2 Alan is ....

 3 Hannah is ....

 4 Eric is ....

 5 Harry is ....

 6 Patricia is ....

 7 Chris is ....

 8 Polly is ....

23 **2** Match the beginnings and endings of the sentences. Then listen and check.

1 Ernie does things quickly and well.
2 Ian has a lot of ideas.
3 Keira always has something nice to say.
4 Irene doesn't need other people to help her.
5 Holly always tells the truth.
6 Ralph does the things he has to do.

a) She's very independent.
b) She's very honest.
c) He's very imaginative.
d) He's really efficient.
e) He's very responsible.
f) She's very kind.

Get talking Talking about personalities and jobs

teacher
doctor
waiter
salesperson
police officer
web designer
nurse
writer

3 Work with a partner. Talk about the jobs listed on the right. Use the adjectives from Exercise 1. Say what you think.

> **A** I think a police officer needs to be honest.

> **B** I agree. And responsible, too. What about a teacher?

Grammar

be going to / present continuous (review)

1 Here are four sentences from the text on page 34. Which sentences:
a talk about someone's intentions? b talk about fixed arrangements for the future?

1 I'm **going to be** a dancer.
2 I'm **going to enjoy** every minute.
3 Next summer **I'm taking** lessons in Flamenco dancing.
4 I'm **going to make** a lot of money.

2 Match the sentences with the pictures.

1 He's going to play soccer. ☐
2 He's playing soccer on Monday. ☐
3 She's going to have lunch. ☐
4 She's having lunch with Jimmy tomorrow. ☐

OK, Jimmy. See you at noon tomorrow for lunch.

3 Write sentences.

1 John / do / homework
John's going to do his homework.

2 Sandra / watch / DVD
....
....

3 They / wash / dog
....
....

4 We / have / picnic
....
....

5 My sister / be / ballet dancer
....
....

6 He / join / army.
....
....

4 Choose some things to do tonight and on the weekend. Write them down.
Work with a partner. Ask and answer questions.

Are you going to a dance club on Sunday?

No, I'm not. I'm staying at home. What about you?

Future time clauses

5 **Match the beginnings and endings of the sentences.**

A	B
1 As soon as I graduate,	a) I'll be a better dancer.
2 When I join the army,	b) I'll help to protect people.
3 After I finish the Flamenco lessons,	c) I'll visit foreign countries.

6 **Look at the phrases in column A in Exercise 5. Circle the correct words below to complete the sentences.**

1 The phrases talk about actions in *the present / the future*.
2 In the phrases, the verb is in the *present / future* tense.

7 **Match the beginnings and endings of the sentences below.**

1 Please turn the lights off before
2 I'll tell her as soon as
3 I'll leave school when
4 I'll do my homework as soon as
5 He wants to join the army after
6 We'll talk about it when

a) she gets here.
b) this show's over.
c) you go home.
d) he graduates.
e) I get home.
f) I'm 16.

8 **Circle the correct word and complete the text.**

When I ¹ (leave) / will leave home, I think I ² go / will go to Canada for a while. Why? Well, I ³ want / will want to see the world before I ⁴ start / will start work. I think I ⁵ go / will go to Toronto. My friend told me that if I ⁶ stay / will stay in small hotels and camp sites, it ⁷ isn't / won't be very expensive. Well, I'm not so sure! But I ⁸ check / will check things out before I ⁹ go / will go. But I know I'm going, and as soon as I ¹⁰ arrive / will arrive in Canada, I ¹¹ go / will go straight to Niagara Falls. That's always been my dream!

9 **Complete with *will ('ll)* and the verb at the end of the sentence.**

1 I.'ll.call.. you as soon as I ..get.. my test scores. (call / get)
2 I don't think it .... before we .... home. (rain / get)
3 I .... over to your place when I .... my homework. (come / finish)
4 As soon as I .... home, I .... a job in a bank. (leave / get)
5 When my parents .... on vacation next week, I .... the house to myself. (go / have)
6 I .... you back when my parents .... me my allowance. (pay / give)

Skills

Reading

1 **Read the magazine article and find the answers to these questions.**

1 How many hours a day does Lena work?
2 How many days a week does she work?

❧❧❧ *Life at Camp America ...* ❧❧❧

Hi, my name's Lena Diekmann. I'm 19 and I'm from Berlin in Germany. I work five days a week at a summer camp in Pennsylvania. I'm a camp counselor. I really like my job because no two days are ever the same. The kids I work with are great and I've made a lot of friends. Anyway, this is my day.

Mornings

I start work very early. I usually wake up at about 6:30 a.m. That's the worst part of my day. I hate getting up that early, but I do it because I have to be awake before any of our campers wake up. I sleep in a cabin with four other counselors. We start work at 7:00 a.m., when we go and help our campers get ready. We have breakfast at 8:00. This is followed by an outdoor activity every morning. Every day of the week we do a different activity such as horseback riding or hiking. I take a break from 12:00-1:00 p.m.

Afternoons

Every afternoon I help teach gymnastics and swimming. I teach gymnastics from 1:00 p.m. until 3:00 and then I teach

swimming until 5:00. I help teach kids who are 10–12 years old. Teaching gymnastics is a lot of fun. But I can't stand swimming because the pool isn't heated and the water is too cold! I like to teach though. It gives me a chance to practice my English, which is why I'm here in the first place!

Evenings

I love the evenings, when everyone at the camp eats a meal together. We laugh and talk about the day's activities. Sometimes we have a campfire. We sing campfire songs. Then the children go to sleep at 8:30 p.m. Even though I'm tired, after that I like to sit around the campfire and talk to my new friends.

All in a day's work!

Working in a camp is a lot of fun.

❧❧❧❧❧❧❧❧❧❧❧❧❧

2 **Read the article again and decide if the sentences are T (True) or F (False).**

1	Lena thinks her job is kind of boring sometimes.	T / F
2	She likes all the people she works with.	T / F
3	Lena sleeps in a cabin.	T / F
4	Lena has to work hard.	T / F
5	Lena teaches gymnastics in the morning.	T / F
6	Lena loves the evenings.	T / F
7	She is tired at the end of the day.	T / F
8	Lena likes campfires.	T / F

Listening

24 **3** **Listen to Kelly and Lee talking about their job interviews. Answer the questions.**

Who:
1 had a good interview?
2 took a dog to the interview?
3 wants to work for a newspaper?
4 has worked as a salesclerk?
5 wants to be a receptionist?
6 wants to start working very soon?
7 said they like working with people?
8 works for the school newspaper?

25 **4** **Listen again and match the questions and answers.**

1 Who is Rover?
2 Why did Kelly take a dog to the interview?
3 What did the interviewer think about the dog?
4 What was Kelly's best answer?
5 Why is Lee happy?
6 What question did the interviewer ask Lee?
7 When did Lee say he could start work?
8 What is Lee waiting for?

a) On Monday.
b) A phone call.
c) Kelly's dog.
d) Your company has an excellent reputation.
e) He didn't seem very happy.
f) Because he had a good interview.
g) Because she had to take him to the vet before.
h) Have you ever worked for a newspaper?

Writing

5 **Complete the text using the words on the left.**

get down
window
wanted
ladder
outside
job

My brother is a window washer. He likes his
¹................... . He likes working ²................... and he loves talking to people. Yesterday he was cleaning a ³................... when a woman next door called over to him. Her cat had climbed a tree and couldn't ⁴................... . He got his ⁵................... and climbed up and got the cat. The woman was very happy and ⁶................... to give my brother some money. Of course my brother wouldn't take it.

6 **Think of someone in your family. Write a short text about his or her job.**

Check your progress Units 3 and 4

1 Complete the sentences.

1 We sometimes go w_ _ _ _ _ shopping when we don't have any money.
2 You shouldn't w_ _ _ _ your money on things you don't need.
3 I bought a s_ _ _ _ _ _ _ _ _ computer because the new ones were too expensive.
4 He won a lot of money and went on a shopping s_ _ _ _.
5 He broke my b_ _ _ _-new laptop!
6 Ian always pays by d_ _ _ _ card. ☐ 6

2 Read the descriptions and complete the sentences.

1 She can make amazing things.
   She's c_ _ _ _ _ _ _.
2 He wants to succeed in life.
   He's a _ _ _ _ _ _ _ _ _.
3 John's really relaxed and nothing bothers him!
   He's e_ _ _ _ _ _ _ _.
4 Anna is always busy and she never takes a break.
   She's h_ _ _ _ _ _ _ _ _ _.
5 Tony doesn't mind waiting for things.
   He's very p_ _ _ _ _ _.
6 Barbara always says "please" and "thank you."
   She's very p_ _ _ _ _. ☐ 6

3 Complete the dialogues. Use the present continuous.

A I'm ¹........... (see) my cousin today.
B What time?
A The train is ²........... (arrive) at 3:00 p.m.
B ³........... (meet) him at the train station?
A Yes, I ⁴........... (take) a taxi there.
B ⁵........... (he/come) alone?
A No, my aunt ⁶........... (come) with him, too. We ⁷........... (have) lunch at The Cedars tomorrow. Do you want to come?
B No, I'm sorry, I ⁸........... (do) my homework! ☐ 8

4 Complete the sentences with the correct verb or word for the future time clause.

1 As .... as he ....(arrive), we'll go.
2 She .... (leave) home .... she is 18.
3 We will go swimming ....we .... (finish) work. ☐ 6

5 Give advice in the following situations.

1 I have to pay a big cell phone bill.
   (not / make so many calls / cell phone)
   You ....
2 I want to become a doctor. (study hard)
   You ....
3 My friend is going to live in Italy.
   (learn / Italian) She ....
4 I have to get up early for work tomorrow.
   (go / bed) You ....
5 My brother isn't feeling well.
   (see / doctor) He .... ☐ 10

6 Complete the sentences with the gerund or infinitive of the verbs in parentheses.

1 I don't like .... alone. (be)
2 There's nothing I love more than .... in the rain. (walk)
3 Gill loves .... (skate)
4 I'm going .... a movie tonight. (see)
5 I want .... a job that involves traveling. (do)
6 Is .... too much ice cream bad for you? (eat)
7 I think you ought .... sorry. (say)
8 Emma hates .... for buses. (wait) ☐ 8

7 Circle the correct answer.

1 I *am going to be / am being* a pilot.
2 Mom, *I'm going / I will go* out tonight. Is that all right?
3 You spent all your money? How are you *buying / going to buy* food for tomorrow?
4 Try to come to my party. Everyone is *going to be / being* there.
5 Read this book—*you're going to like it / you're liking it.*
6 I think you ought to *say / saying* you're sorry. ☐ 6

TOTAL ☐ 50

My progress so far is ...

☺ ☺ ☹
great! ☐   good. ☐   poor. ☐

Park rangers

1 Read about a park ranger's job.

Do you know?

Yellowstone National Park is known for its geysers such as Old Faithful, its hot springs, and bubbly activity. All these features point to the fact that Yellowstone is one of the world's largest active volcanoes! But don't fear, the last major eruption here took place about 640,000 years ago.

Yellowstone National Park

Established in 1872, Yellowstone National Park covers more than 8,900 square kilometers in the states of Wyoming, Montana, and Idaho. Millions of people visit the park each year. It features nine visitor centers and 12 campgrounds with more than 2,000 campsites, and it is patrolled by 49 year-round rangers and hundreds of part-time summer rangers.

Backcountry rangers

Around 98 percent of Yellowstone is "backcountry." There are just 22 backcountry rangers who patrol and maintain the park's many trails on foot, skis, or horseback. They monitor wildlife and help enforce rules and safety regulations with the public who use the backcountry areas of the park.

Patrol rangers

Yellowstone's "front country" includes all its developed areas, including roads. Patrol rangers help to enforce traffic rules. They patrol all the roads within the park and work to prevent car accidents in Yellowstone. Every year there are around 600 car accidents and 100 animals killed on the roads in the park.

Other rangers

Yellowstone also has many other rangers, too. They work in the entrance booths, museums, visitor centers, or spend time educating the public about the park.

Rewards

Many of the rangers who work in Yellowstone only work during the summer months. Few work in full-time positions, and the work is not very well paid. But rangers love what they do. Most would say that they're not in it for the money!

26

2 Dick is talking about ranger jobs. Listen and circle T (True) or F (False).

1 You normally have to have a college degree to become a park ranger. T / F
2 Dick has been a park ranger for 20 years. T / F
3 Dick's first job in the park was backcountry ranger. T / F
4 Dick fell in love with the outdoors on visits to his uncle's ranch. T / F
5 Park rangers rarely work in the same park for their entire career. T / F

3 Do you have a part-time job? Do you know anyone with an unusual or special job? Tell the class about them.

4 **Over 2 U!** Who works in the parks in your country? Find out about their job or another job and write a description. Use Exercise 1 to help you.

American MORE! Now you can watch Episode 2 of *School Reporters!*

Omelets and hard work: A recipe for success

On his first day in the U.S. in 1990, George Wannous lost all his money. George had left Syria, his home country, because a friend who had moved from Syria to Sacramento, California, invited him to come to the U.S. and work on a fruit farm. But George never got as far as Sacramento.

When the 19-year-old Syrian landed at Los Angeles airport, he took a bus to the center of town so he could get a train to Sacramento. When he got off the bus, a man approached him and took out a knife. He pointed it at George. "The man took all my money, everything I had," George says. "It was awful."

George went to the police and two police officers felt sorry for him. They gave him a small amount of money and put him on a train to Sacramento.

For some reason, George got off the train in San Francisco, and the next day he started to look for a job. First he went to work at a bakery, but at the same time he took other jobs, too. He worked very hard. For half a year, he sold bread in the morning and in the afternoon he cleaned offices for minimum wage. For awhile, he also worked as a taxi driver at night. In 1993, he got a job as a dishwasher in a small café. The manager of the café liked George. He told him to study the menu carefully so he could become a waiter. "All the food on the menu was new to me," George says. "A medium-rare hamburger! In my country we cook everything well-done." George became a waiter, slowly worked his way up, and half a year later he became the manager of the café.

When the owner decided to sell the café, George went to the bank to borrow money to buy it. He started to work extremely hard—up to 20 hours a day! When he was tired, he slept in his car in the parking lot.

That was 11 years ago. George has become successful. He is very smart. Instead of making three-egg omelets as the old company did, he uses four eggs. George says. "My friends told me I would lose money selling bigger omelets for the same price. But I didn't lose money. I got happier customers—and more customers."

George is 39 now. He's happily married and he has three children. He has a much bigger café now, and there are eight people working for him. George has made it, thanks to his hard work!

For **MORE!** Go to **www.cambridge.org/elt/americanmore** and take a quiz on this text.

UNIT (5) Bookworms

In this unit

You learn
- *so / such*
- phrasal verbs
- words for kinds of books

and then you can
- give reasons
- talk about books

27 **1** **Listen and read.**

Juan Hey Emily, I'm bored. Let's go and hang out at the mall.

Emily Can't you see I'm reading a book?

Juan Come on. You can finish it later.

Emily I'm sorry. It's such a good book—I can't put it down.

Juan What are you reading anyway?

Emily It's a book by Scott Westerfeld. It's called *Uglies*.

Juan *Uglies*? What's it about?

Emily Do you really want to know? Or are you just bored?

Juan How can you say such a thing? Of course I'm interested. Honestly.

Emily Well, OK. So it all takes place in the future. All kids are "Uglies" until they're 16. Then they have an operation and turn into "Pretties."

Pretties are good-looking. They mess around and have parties all the time.

Juan That sounds like fun.

Emily Yeah, but it's not what it seems. There's this rebel group of kids who run away to escape the operation. It's called "The Smoke." The government is after them before they find out the truth. It's all very exciting.

Juan It all seems very confusing to me.

Emily Yeah, but if you start reading it you'll get into it, I promise.

Juan You know, I'm so bored I might just do that. Hand over the book.

Emily No way! You'll have to hang on until I finish!

2 **Match the sentence halves to make a summary of the dialogue.**

1	Juan wants	a) reading her book.
2	Emily is happy	b) what "Uglies" become after an operation.
3	*Uglies* is	c) take the book from Emily.
4	"Pretties" are	d) Juan should read the book.
5	Juan thinks	e) about teenage life in the future.
6	Emily says	f) the book sounds confusing.
7	Juan tries to	g) to do something.

Get talking Giving reasons

28

3 **Write the answers under the questions. Listen and check.**

1 It was so good I didn't want it to end.
2 It was so exciting I couldn't put it down.
3 It was so noisy I couldn't talk to anyone.
4 It was so long I slept most of the way.

A How was the book?

....

C How was your vacation?

....

B How was the drive?

....

D How was the party?

....

4 **Work with a partner. Student A chooses a picture to ask about.**
Student B chooses prompts from the A and B boxes to reply.

A How was the movie? **B** It was so boring that I walked out of the movie theater.

movie

roller coaster

pizza

test

beach

hotel bed

A	B
boring	walk out of the movie theater
comfortable	get a headache
exciting	want another piece
hot	not want to get out of it
delicious	try again immediately
difficult	spend all the time in the water

Language Focus

Vocabulary Kinds of books

1 **Match the kinds of books with the titles.**

1 a detective novel
2 a biography
3 poetry
4 short stories
5 nonfiction
6 a book about animals
7 a comic book
8 a romance

a) *The Collected Poems of Whitman*
b) *Love in the Spring*
c) *Tears of a Clown and Other Stories*
d) *Ordinary Genius: The Story of Albert Einstein*
e) *Taking Care of Your Horse*
f) *How to Write Better*
g) *The Body in the Library*
h) *Batman Returns*

Get talking Talking about books

2 **Put the lines in order to make two dialogues. Listen and check.** (29)

1 A ☐ So what do you like?
A ☐ Do you like poetry?
B ☐ It's OK, but it's not my favorite.
B ☐ I sort of like short stories, but I love comic books.

2 C ☐ So what do you like books about?
C ☐ Do you like books about horses?
D ☐ Horses? No, I don't.
D ☐ Football and cars.

3 **Work with a partner. Say what you think about the kinds of books in Exercise 1.**

4 **Look at the books. What kind of book do you think each one is?**

   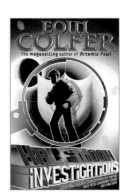

5 **Which of these books looks interesting to you? If you had to pick one, which one would it be and why?**

I'd pick … because it looks interesting / funny / thrilling / exciting…
I'd pick it, because I like thrillers / love / horror / sci-fi stories…
I'd pick it because I've already read … by the same author.

Grammar

So / such

1 Look at the examples and complete the rule.

*It's **such** a good book (that) I can't put it down.*
*I'm **so** bored (that) I might just do that.*

Rule

We can use [1].......... before a noun and [2]........... before an adjective to emphasize the quality of the noun or adjective. We can also talk about the result by adding *that* followed by a clause.

2 Match the pictures and sentences.

1 It was such a hot day that we went swimming.
2 I was so bored that I watched TV all day.
3 It was so hot that I burned my mouth.
4 I was feeling so energetic that I went for a swim.
5 I was so thirsty that I drank the whole glass at once.
6 It was such a scary movie that I couldn't watch.
7 The sun was so bright that I had to wear sunglasses.
8 I have such bad eyesight that I have to wear glasses.

3 Circle the correct word.

1 The movie was *such / so* long that I fell asleep.
2 I had *such / so* a bad dream that I couldn't get back to sleep.
3 The accident was *such / so* serious that they called a helicopter ambulance.
4 The lake was *such / so* dirty that we didn't go in it.
5 I have *such / so* a bad headache that I'm going to bed.
6 That's *such / so* a great idea, I just might do it.

4 Rewrite the two sentences to make one single sentence. Use the word in parentheses.

1 I was really hungry. I ordered another sandwich. (so)
   I was so hungry that I ordered another sandwich.
2 The test was really difficult. I didn't pass it. (such) ....
3 The computer was very expensive. I couldn't afford it. (so) ....
4 The view was really beautiful. I had to take a photo. (such) ....
5 He speaks really fast. I don't understand a word he says. (so) ....
6 The game was really good. I didn't want it to end. (such) ....

Phrasal verbs

(5) **Look at the dialogue on page 44 and complete the sentences below.**

Let's go and ¹.................... at the mall.
Then they have an operation and ².................... "Pretties."
They ³.................... and have parties all the time.
The government is after them before they ⁴.................... the truth.
If you start reading it, you'll ⁵.................... it, I promise.
You'll have to ⁶.................... until I finish!

(6) **Match the phrasal verbs in Exercise 5 with these definitions.**

1 become   ....   4 have fun   ....
2 discover   ....   5 spend some time   ....
3 start to enjoy a lot ....   6 wait   ....

(7) **The following contain verbs with prepositions. How are they different from phrasal verbs?**

There's this rebel group of kids who *run away* to escape the operation.
It's such a good book I can't *put* it *down*.

Many verbs in English are followed by prepositions. Sometimes this verb-preposition structure can't be immediately understood by looking at the individual words. These are called phrasal verbs.

(8) **Circle the phrasal verbs in the sentences below. What do they mean?**

1   He really takes after his father. They like all the same things.
2   I'm sorry. I've just knocked over your glass of water.
3   Paul, stand up and come here.
4   Guess who I ran into today in town? Josh, I haven't seen him for years.
5   Can you turn up the volume? I can't hear a thing.
6   I've taken up judo. I'm not very good yet, but it's just the beginning.
7   I lent Max my bike and told him to take care of it.
8   The teacher told us not to play around.
9   I don't know how much it costs, but I'll look into it.
10 I ran after the bus, but I couldn't catch it.

(9) **Complete the sentences with the phrasal verbs on this page.**

1   She really .... her mother.
2   It's a great game. You'll really .... it.
3   Kiss me and I'll .... a prince, I promise.
4   You'll have to .... for awhile. The firefighters are coming.
5   He's just .... yoga, so he's still got a lot to learn.
6   It was really nice to .... you. I haven't seen you for such a long time.

48   UNIT 5

Skills

Reading

1 **Read the book review. Does Brenda like the book?**

Saving the world one mission at a time

ALEX RIDER
CROCODILE TEARS

ANTHONY HOROWITZ
#1 New York Times bestselling author

Hi, this is Brenda's Books online. This week the book I'm recommending is one I've been waiting to read for ages—and it's been well worth the wait. It is the latest spy adventure by Anthony Horowitz—*Crocodile Tears: An Alex Rider Novel*. I've been a big fan of Alex Rider, a teenage spy, ever since the first novel, *Stormbreaker*. This is the eighth book in the series and they just keep getting better.

For any of you who have never read an Alex Rider novel, Horowitz's hero is a kind of junior James Bond who works for MI6, but he's much cooler than James Bond and his missions are more dangerous. *Crocodile Tears* starts off with an explosion at a nuclear power station in India. The action then moves to Scotland where Alex is on vacation, to London, and then to Kenya. The book is full of action, and Alex faces a variety of dangerous situations as he deals with his latest adversary. But does he sort out his problems and save the world? Well, I know the answer because I've read the book but I'm not telling you. All I can promise is that you won't be disappointed. It's fast and exciting with action on every page. It's impossible to put down. I read it in two sittings and that's only because my mom insisted that I eat dinner with my family right in the middle of it.

Horowitz explains, "I think this has probably got more action in it than any other Alex Rider book so far. It's a little bit longer than normal and there are more action sequences."

2 **Circle T (True) or F (False) for the sentences below.**

1 Brenda was already a fan of the Alex Rider books. T / F
2 There have been four books between *Stormbreaker* and *Crocodile Tears*. T / F
3 Brenda thinks *Crocodile Tears* is the best of the Alex Rider books. T / F
4 Alex Rider works with James Bond. T / F
5 Alex is on vacation in Scotland. T / F
6 Brenda didn't finish the book in one sitting. T / F
7 Brenda thinks there's not enough action in the book. T / F

Listening

3 **Listen to Julie, Fred, and Farid talking about what they think of reading and about their favorite books. Answer the questions with their names.**

Who...
1 prefers TV to books?
2 loves reading
3 is reading a book about a movie?
4 likes horror stories?
5 reads two or three books every month?
6 likes fantasy stories
7 likes books for teenage girls?

Speaking and listening

4 Read the beginning of the Alex Rider book *Snakehead*. Check the picture it describes.

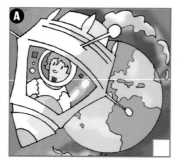  

Splash down.

Alex Rider would never forget the moment of impact, the first shock as the parachute opened and the second—more jolting still—as the module that had carried him back from outer space crashed into the sea. Was it his imagination or was there steam rising up all around him? Maybe it was sea spray. It didn't matter. He was back. That was all he cared about. He had made it. He was still alive.

He was lying on his back, crammed into the tiny capsule with his knees tucked into his chest. Half closing his eyes, Alex experienced a moment of extraordinary stillness. He was motionless. His fists were clenched. He wasn't breathing. Already he found it impossible to believe that the events that had led to his journey into space had really taken place. He tried to imagine himself hurtling around the earth at seventeen and a half thousand miles an hour. It couldn't have happened. It had surely all been part of some incredible dream.

5 Find these words in the text and circle the best definition for each one.

1 jolting
   a) moving in a sudden, strong way   b) quiet   c) in a relaxed way
2 module
   a) a parachute   b) part of a spaceship   c) a small boat
3 crammed
   a) with not much room   b) with a lot of room   c) asleep
4 clenched fist
   a) 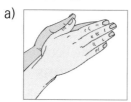   b) 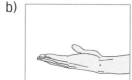   c)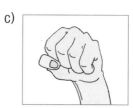

5 hurtling
a) moving slowly   b) moving quickly   c) moving really quickly

6 *"Already he found it impossible to believe that the events that had led to his journey into space had really taken place."*
Work with a partner. Decide what those events may have been. Make up a short story. Tell your story to the rest of the class and vote on the best one.

Speaking and writing

7 Think of the last book you read and write notes to answer the questions.

- *Title / author?*
- *What kind of book is it?*
- *What's it about?*
- *Did you like it? Why/why not?*

8 Work with a partner. Ask and answer questions about your books.

9 Read the review below and answer the questions.

1 What happens in the book?
2 Did Anahita like it? (Why/why not?)

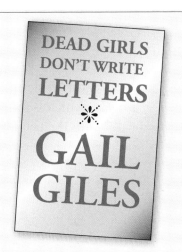

- Book: Dead Girls Don't Write Letters
- Author: Gail Giles
- What's it about?

Sunny's sister Jazz (who is NOT a nice girl) dies in a fire. Her parents are really sad, but one day Sunny gets a letter from Jazz. "I'll be coming home soon," it says. And in fact, one day Jazz turns up. She has turned into a nice, friendly girl, and she knows everything about the family's past. But Sunny asks herself a big question: Who is this stranger who says she's Jazz? She knows that dead girls can't write letters!

- What do I think of it?

Wow! This is really a good book. It's so exciting and full of twists. I liked the idea that the sisters are so different (aren't they often in real life?) and that suddenly the bad one is good. What do you do if you've always been the good one? I won't tell you the ending, but I can tell you that there are a couple of surprises. And have a look at Giles' next book. It's called Playing in Traffic, and it's a thriller, too.
(Review by Anahita)

10 Expand your notes from Exercise 7 and write a book report. Use the model above to help you.

Sounds right Stress in compound nouns

31 **11** In compound words, the stress is normally on the first syllable in the word. Underline the syllable that is stressed in the words below. Then listen and check.

comic book   horror story   poetry book   science fiction

Migration

Key words

migrate	breeding grounds	current	Arctic tern
migratory animals/birds	predators	salmon	ruby-throated
breed	supply	blue whale	hummingbird

1 **Read the article and match the headings to the paragraphs.**

1 24-hour sunlight
2 North and south
3 The final journey
4 Size isn't important
5 Flying through water

A ☐

Each year, blue whales travel thousands of kilometers in search of food. They spend the winter months in the warm waters of the tropics where many of them give birth to their young. When summer arrives, some of them migrate south to Antarctica, and others go north to the Arctic. All of them are looking for the rich supply of plankton which is found in polar waters. After three or four months of feeding, they swim back to the tropics.

B ☐

Pacific salmon are famous for their difficult journeys of hundreds of kilometers from the ocean to their breeding grounds up American rivers. When they start the journey, their bodies are very strong, but as soon as the salmon leave the ocean, they stop eating.

They swim upriver, fighting against strong currents and jumping up waterfalls. Many are eaten by predators or caught by fishermen. Months later, the lucky ones arrive, but they are exhausted. They have just enough energy to lay their eggs before they die.

c ☐

Arctic terns fly an incredible 40,000 km every year as they travel between the North and South poles. They also probably see more daylight than any other animal on Earth. In their northern home during the summer, the sun doesn't set, and they experience the same long days in their winter home in Antarctica.

D ☐

They may only weigh a couple of grams, but when it comes to long-distance flying, ruby-throated hummingbirds are big birds. Twice a year, these amazing creatures take off from the U.S. on a 2,400-km journey before they finally land in Costa Rica. This journey includes a 960-km, 20-hour nonstop flight across the Gulf of Mexico.

E ☐

They can't fly but that doesn't stop penguins from getting around. They are the only birds that migrate by swimming. Using currents, they can migrate from Antarctica as far up the east coast of South America as Rio de Janeiro in Brazil.

Mini-project Research on migratory birds

2 **Choose one of these birds.**

stork   wild goose   starling   crane   puffin

Search the Internet or a library for information about their migration. Think about the questions below. Write a short paragraph to answer each question.

Where do they live?
Where do they migrate to?
Why do they migrate?
How far do they travel?
What dangers are there on their journey?

Biology

UNIT 5   53

1 Listen and read.

In this unit

You learn
- the passive
- *make / let / be allowed to*
- words for special events

and then you can
- talk about permission
- talk about events
- say what people let you do

Tennis anyone?

From the U.S. Open to Wimbledon, kids around the world work hard to make tennis tournaments come alive.

My name is Sheri and I'm a huge tennis fan. I always wanted to experience a Grand Slam tournament. Every year, there are four Grand Slam events—the Australian Open, the French Open, the U.S. Open, and Wimbledon. And last year I got to go to one of them and watch the best tennis players in the world play—for free. How? I became a ball girl at the U.S. Open!

Each year about 270 ball girls and boys are chosen to work at the U.S. Open. Many ball boys and girls come back year after year, but some teenagers try out for the role, too.

Last year, 300 of us tried out for 70 ball-person positions. The tryouts lasted for two exhausting months. "What?" I can hear you thinking, "Two-month-long tryouts? What's so difficult about picking up tennis balls?" Sorry, but you really have no idea! When we first applied, they made us run for 12 minutes, and then stand completely still for four minutes! Does that sound easy? Try it sometime!

Being a ball boy or girl can be dangerous, too. A few years ago at Wimbledon, for example, a ball boy was hit by a 200 kph serve from Pete Sampras, the champion at the time, but the ball boy just smiled and kept going!

Anyway, in the end I was selected, so I went to the U.S. Open and did my stuff. It was great! It was so exciting to be so close to some of my favorite players. I couldn't talk to them since ball boys and girls aren't allowed to talk to players during the matches. But after the matches ended, players would let us take photographs and ask for autographs.

I wasn't paid any money and I had to work hard, but I had an amazing two weeks. I'm hoping that I can go back and be a ball girl again for at least a couple more years!

2 Circle T (True) or F (False) for the sentences below.

1 Sheri is a huge football fan.   T / F
2 She trained for five months to be a ball girl.   T / F
3 Being a ball boy or girl isn't easy.   T / F
4 A ball boy went to the hospital when a ball hit him. T / F
5 Sheri talked to some players during the matches. T / F
6 She doesn't want to be a ball girl again this year. T / F

Get talking Talking about permission

33

3 Match the questions and answers. Then listen and check.

1 Why don't you wear a hat to school?
2 Why weren't you at the party?
3 Why don't you take your cell phone to school?
4 Why isn't there a TV in your bedroom?

a) I wasn't allowed to go.
b) We're not allowed to use them there.
c) I'm not allowed to have one.
d) We're not allowed to wear them.

4 Work with a partner. Use the prompts to make short conversations.

A Are you allowed to .... ?

B Yes, but I'm not allowed to ....

✓ go to parties
✗ come home late

✓ surf the Internet
✗ go into chat rooms

✓ buy your own clothes
✗ dye my hair

✓ invite friends over
✗ make a lot of noise

✓ go to fast-food restaurants
✗ eat fast food every day

Language Focus

Vocabulary Special events

1 **Match the words and pictures.**

- [ ] car show
- [ ] school fair
- [ ] fashion show
- [ ] music festival
- [ ] tennis tournament
- [ ] movie premiere
- [ ] bike race
- [ ] book fair

2 **Where would you expect to find these people?**

actors	fans	teachers	models
athletes	authors	rock stars	journalists

Get talking Talking about events

34 **3** **Complete the dialogues with the replies. Listen and check.**

a) I saw some really cool clothing designs and hair styles.

b) Yes, I went to Lollapalooza last year.

c) Yes, there was one at the mall last year.

d) It was fantastic. All of my favorite bands were there.

A Have you ever been to a rock festival?
B ¹Yes, I went to Lollapalooza last year.
A What was it like?
B ² ....

A Have you ever been to a fashion show?
B ³ ....
A What was it like?
B ⁴ ....

4 **Work with a partner. Ask each other questions about the events in Exercise 1. Use the dialogues from Exercise 3 to help you.**

Grammar

The passive

1 Complete the sentences from the text on page 54 with the words on the right.

1 Each year ball boys and girls ....
2 A ball boy .... by a 200 kph serve.
3 Ball boys and girls .... to talk to players.
4 I .... any money.

> was hit
> are chosen
> aren't allowed
> wasn't paid

The simple present passive has the following structure:
Subject + simple present of **be (not) + past participle**.

The simple past passive has the following structure:
Subject + simple past of **be (not) + past participle**.

2 Read the sentences. Which events from Exercise 1 on page 56 are they talking about?

1 The movie is shown to a specially invited audience.
2 The cars are washed every morning.
3 The parents of the children are all invited.
4 The race leader wears a yellow shirt.
5 The champion wins $500,000.
6 Bands from all over the U.S. come to play.

3 Complete the sentences with the simple present passive form of the verb.

How it works: A rock festival
1 First a big field .... (find) for the event.
2 Then the bands .... (choose) and .... (invite) to play.
3 The festival .... (advertise) on the radio and in newspapers.
4 Tickets .... (sold) on the Internet.
5 A big stage .... (build) in the field.
6 Security .... (arrange).
7 The gates .... (open).
8 Finally the fans .... (search) when they arrive.

4 Rewrite the underlined sentences. Use the past passive.

The school fashion show was a great success. [1]They invited 100 people and most of them came. [2]They raised more than $1,000 for charity. It really was a big event and there were even a few local celebrities there. [3]The photographers took tons of pictures and [4]the newspaper put the show on its front page. The clothes were great. [5]Teenagers designed them all. It was amazing. In fact, [6]the teenagers planned the whole evening. [7]A 16-year-old boy wrote the music and [8]a 14-year-old girl did the lights. It was amazing to see what a group of teenagers can do.

1 100 people ..*were invited.*..
2 More than $1,000 ....
3 Tons of pictures ....
4 The show ....
5 All the clothes ....
6 ....
7 ....
8 ....

Make / let / be allowed to

5 **Complete the sentences from the text on page 54. Use *made / let / allowed.***

1 They .... us run for 12 minutes.
2 Ball boys and girls aren't .... to talk to players during the matches.
3 Players would .... us take photographs.

Note
The past tense of *let* is *let*.

6 **Nick is at a camp. Write sentences starting with *They make him / don't make him / let him / don't let him...***

1 make / get up / six o'clock every morning
   They make him get up at six o'clock every morning.
2 not let / stay up later than 10:00 p.m.
3 make / help serve the food
4 not make / help with the cleaning
5 let / watch football on TV
6 make / put up his own tent
7 not let / stay in the tent during the day
8 let / use the Internet in the camp office

7 **Match the signs and the sentences.**

1 You aren't allowed to keep the lights on after 11:00 p.m.
2 Dogs aren't allowed.
3 You aren't allowed to walk on the grass.
4 You aren't allowed to feed the animals.
5 You aren't allowed to run.
6 You aren't allowed to use cell phones.

8 **Write sentences using the correct form of *be allowed to.***

1 James ✓ watch TV / ✗ watch TV after 10 o'clock.
   James is allowed to watch TV, but he isn't allowed to watch TV after 10 o'clock.
2 Sarah ✓ go to bed late / ✗ get up late
   ....
3 We ✓ wear jeans to school / ✗ wear shorts
   ....
4 They ✓ listen to music / ✗ listen without headphones
   ....
5 I ✓ go to my friend's house / ✗ stay overnight
   ....
6 She ✓ have parties at home / ✗ play loud music
   ....

Skills

Reading

1 **Read the magazine article. Find out what these numbers refer to.**

a) more than 3 million   b) 200,000   c) between 1 and 2 million   d) 5,000

Really big events? Rio's the place!

Soccer crowds

The largest number of people ever at a soccer game was in 1950 at the final of the Soccer World Cup at the Maracanã Stadium in Rio de Janeiro. The stadium was built for the World Cup, and everyone in Brazil was sure that Brazil would win. They went to see the final against Uruguay, and only needed a tie to be the champions. A total of 173,850 people paid to go in and watch, but journalists and officials made the number 200,000 or so. But, to the disappointment of the Brazilians, Uruguay won 2–1 to take the World Cup for the second time.

Rock concerts

There have been some enormous rock concerts in Rio. In 1994, Rod Stewart played on the beach in Copacabana on December 31, and it is estimated that more than 3 million people were there—a world record. The Rolling Stones played on the beach just before Rio Carnival in 2006, but they only(!) got about 1.2 million people to come and watch. And there have been three "Rock in Rio" festivals, with hundreds of thousands of fans going over three or four days to watch bands such as R.E.M. and Red Hot Chili Peppers.

Carnival

The number of people at Rio Carnival is difficult to measure, at least if you're thinking about the number of people in the streets of Rio. But one thing is for sure: the parade of samba schools in the Sambódromo is huge. Each year, during two consecutive nights, the 14 top samba schools in Rio parade through the stadium. Each school has between 4,000 and 5,000 people, and each school takes 80 minutes to parade. The special stadium, which was built in 1984, holds 65,000 people, but millions of people watch on TV, too.

New Year's Eve

New Year's Eve is a big event almost everywhere in the world, but there are very few places where it's bigger than Copacabana in Rio de Janeiro. Usually there are between 1 and 2 million people on the beach to watch the fireworks that begin at midnight. These days, after the fireworks there are usually two or three simultaneous concerts on the beach with famous musicians. The party goes on, of course, into the daylight hours!

2 **Read the text again. Answer the questions.**

1 Why was the Maracanã Stadium built?
2 Why were the Brazilians disappointed in 1950?
3 Who takes part in the parades in the Sambódromo each year?
4 How many people can watch the samba school parade in the Sambódromo?
5 How long do "Rock in Rio" festivals last?
6 What time does the New Year's Eve party finish?

Listening

3 Say the numbers in the table.

20	312,000	687	42,000
140,000	500,000	27,000	2 billion

35

Where do you think the numbers go in the text below? Fill in the blanks, and then listen and check.

Total number of spectators: [1].......................... (40,000 people a day)
Amount of strawberries: [2]..................... kilograms
Number of bottles of water: [3].....................
Number of ice creams: [4].........................
Number of matches: [5]....................
Number of courts: [6]....................
Number of tennis balls: [7].........................
Number of TV viewers: [8]....................

THE CHAMPIONSHIPS
WIMBLEDON

Speaking and listening

36

4 Listen to a group of students discussing the task on the right. Make a note of their answers to the questions.

5 Work in small groups and plan your own event. Present your ideas to the class.

Task: You are going to plan an event to raise money for charity.

1 What kind of event are you going to choose?
2 What things do you need to plan?
3 Who is going to do what?
4 How much money do you want to make?
5 What kind of charity are you going to give it to?

Writing

6 Look at the poster for the rock festival. Write a similar poster for your own event.

11A productions proudly present
King High School Experience
Rock Festival
Featuring:
**The Flying Pigs,
Overdrive,
Skool Rulez, and The Henriettas.**

When: Saturday July 1
Where: School football field
Tickets only $5 for the whole day
See **Leroy Sparks** (11A)

Let us entertain you!

Check your progress Units 5 and 6

1 Complete the words.

1 c_ _ _ _ _ _ _ _
   of short stories
2 rock f_ _ _ _ _ _ _
3 detective n_ _ _ _
4 fashion s_ _ _
5 school f_ _ _

6 tennis
   t_ _ _ _ _ _ _ _
7 nonf_ _ _ _ _ _
   book
8 movie pre_ _ _ _ _

[ ] 8

2 Complete the sentences.

1 It's a comedy, it's _ _ _ _ _ _ .
2 It's a sci-fi, it's _ _ _ _ _ _ _ _ _ .
3 It's a _ _ _ _ _ _ _ _ _ _ , it's interesting.
4 It's a horror story, it's _ _ _ _ _ .
5 It's a _ _ _ _ _ _ _ _ , it's thrilling.

[ ] 5

3 Complete the dialogues. Use the passive (present or past) and *so/such.*

1 **A** This is ¹.............. a good book.
   B Who ².............. it .... (write) by?
   A Philip Pullman. It's great. I'm ³..............
       excited about what happens next.
   B I think that book ⁴.............. (chose) for a
       prize.
   A Yes, it was. He's ⁵.............. a good writer!

2 **A** There's a music festival on the weekend.
       It ⁶....................... (advertise) in the local
       newspaper. There are ⁷....................... a lot
       of famous groups coming!
   B It's ⁸....................... wet though. It might
       not happen.
   A Don't say that! I've already got a ticket!
       The tickets ⁹....................... (sell) online.
   B Were they? I'm ¹⁰....................... terrible
       with computers! I never buy anything
       online.
   A It's not ¹¹....................... a difficult thing to
       do! Come on! I'll help you!

[ ] 11

4 Complete using *so* or *such.*

1 That was .... silly of you.
2 Gina was .... tired that she went
   straight to bed.
3 This is .... an interesting book!
4 I have never seen .... a bad movie!

5 He's going to buy me a book. That's
   .... a great idea!

[ ] 5

5 Complete the phrasal verbs.

1 I .... into your sister at the mall.
2 Oh wow! I love this song! .... it up!
3 Jim's .... up horseback riding. He'd
   never tried it before!
4 Who do you .... after most, your mom
   or your dad?
5 Billy .... over a glass of water onto my
   cell phone!
6 Sometimes I need to read half a book before
   I .... into it.

[ ] 6

6 Rewrite the sentences using the passive.

1 They chose our school to enter the contest.
   ....
2 They always invite parents to the school fair.
   ....
3 A falling light hit a fan at the concert.
   ....
4 They searched the girl.
   ....
5 We plan a party at the end of every year.
   ....

[ ] 10

7 Complete using *make, let,* or *be allowed.*

1 My teachers .... me do too much
   work.
2 I .... to go out tonight. My mom said
   no.
3 They won't .... me watch that movie.
4 She .... me try her new shoes.
5 He .... me to drive his car.

[ ] 5

[TOTAL] [50]

My progress so far is ...

☺   ☺   ☹

great! [ ]   good. [ ]   poor. [ ]

Marathons!

1 Read the text and decide if the sentences below are T (True) or F (False).

1 There are some difficult hills in the San Francisco Marathon. T / F
2 The St. George Marathon is harder than most. T / F
3 Anyone can sign up to run in the Boston Marathon. T / F
4 There is a marathon where you run on ice. T / F
5 In the marathon in the Himalayas, you have to run up Mt. Everest. T / F

Marathons are run everywhere. There are a lot to choose from if you want to see different places. In just about every major city and even in remote places. Perhaps the best-known is the Boston Marathon. It has been taking place for more than 100 years. Runners need to qualify for Boston, so only the best runners participate in this race. Other popular marathons include the scenic (and largely downhill) St. George Marathon in Utah, the Chicago Marathon, and the San Francisco Marathon, which has a few tough hills! There's also the New York City Marathon. With its 39,000 participants, you'd have no shortage of company. For people who want to travel farther, marathons are also held in the North Pole, where you run on ice! There's even a marathon in the Himalayas, but you don't have to run up Mt. Everest!

37 **2** Listen and try to match the people in the New York City Marathon to the charities they supported. Then listen again and check.

Competitor	Charity
Dressed in red tank tops	Maasai Warriors
In yellow jerseys	Fred's Team
As themselves	Team for Kids

Do you know?

Originally, there was no fixed distance for the marathon race. 40 kilometers became the standard until the 1908 Olympic Games in London, when the race was made longer so that members of the royal family could see the start and finish. We use that same distance today—42.195 kilometers.

38 **3** Look at the table below and try to complete the missing times for the Boston Marathon. Then listen and check your answers.

Competitor	Time
Fastest man	[1].... hours [2].... minutes 14 seconds
Fastest woman	[3].... hours [4].... minutes 43 seconds

4 **Over 2 U!** Imagine you are going to take part in a marathon. In groups, decide which charity you'd like to raise money for and design a costume to wear. Find out about that charity. Write a paragraph about it and present it to the class.

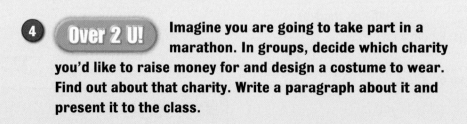
American MORE! Now you can watch Episode 3 of *School Reporters!*

Chill out at Lollapalooza

Want some ideas for things to do in the summer? Here's my highlight from last August. I went to Lollapalooza for three days with my older brother Daniel. What's Lollapalooza? A three-day music festival with eight separate stages and tons of bands. It started on a Friday and lasted for three days. Great bands! I liked The Killers, Jane's Addiction, Kings of Leon, and Vampire Weekend best. It was awesome.

Daniel's been going to Lollapalooza for a couple of years now. He says he's had some great experiences there. Here's an example. The first time Cage the Elephant came to Lollapalooza, they played in a tent with about 1,000 people in it, all standing up. When they'd been playing for some time, people started crowdsurfing. I could never do it, but Daniel launched himself up and was carried along by the crowd. Daniel says it was scary, but like nothing else he'd experienced ever before.

We stayed at an apartment where one of Daniel's friends lives. There were about 12 of us staying there. But all we did was go there to sleep. The next morning we were up to see more music.

Four more things I liked about the weekend:

Number 1. There was a big section of really cool eco-vendors.

Number 2. Grant Park, where the festival's held, is a really cool place in downtown Chicago.

Number 3. There was an autograph booth where you can meet your favorite bands.

Number 4. Last but not least, the toilets were clean (and believe me, at a music festival, that's important!)

So if you want something a little different to do this year, you could try Lollapalooza. Just check out www.lollapalooza.com.

For MORE! Go to www.cambridge.org/elt/americanmore and take a quiz on this text.

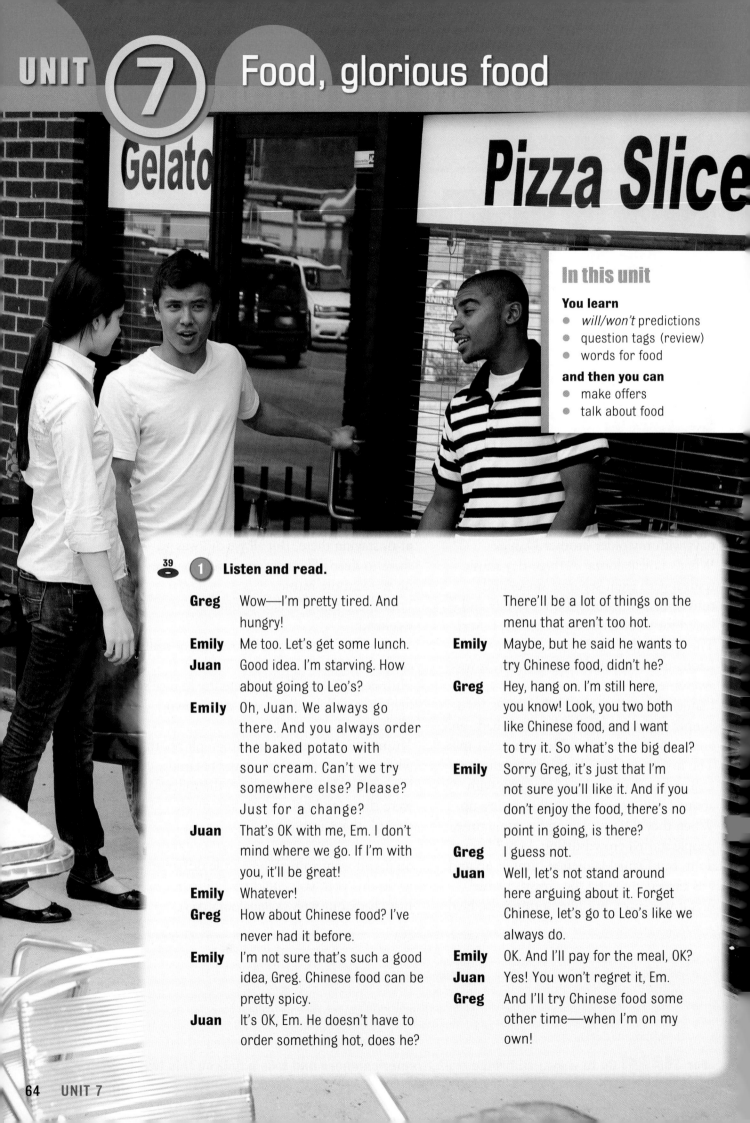

UNIT ⑦ Food, glorious food

Gelato

Pizza Slice

In this unit

You learn
- *will/won't* predictions
- question tags (review)
- words for food

and then you can
- make offers
- talk about food

39

1 **Listen and read.**

Greg Wow—I'm pretty tired. And hungry!

Emily Me too. Let's get some lunch.

Juan Good idea. I'm starving. How about going to Leo's?

Emily Oh, Juan. We always go there. And you always order the baked potato with sour cream. Can't we try somewhere else? Please? Just for a change?

Juan That's OK with me, Em. I don't mind where we go. If I'm with you, it'll be great!

Emily Whatever!

Greg How about Chinese food? I've never had it before.

Emily I'm not sure that's such a good idea, Greg. Chinese food can be pretty spicy.

Juan It's OK, Em. He doesn't have to order something hot, does he?

There'll be a lot of things on the menu that aren't too hot.

Emily Maybe, but he said he wants to try Chinese food, didn't he?

Greg Hey, hang on. I'm still here, you know! Look, you two both like Chinese food, and I want to try it. So what's the big deal?

Emily Sorry Greg, it's just that I'm not sure you'll like it. And if you don't enjoy the food, there's no point in going, is there?

Greg I guess not.

Juan Well, let's not stand around here arguing about it. Forget Chinese, let's go to Leo's like we always do.

Emily OK. And I'll pay for the meal, OK?

Juan Yes! You won't regret it, Em.

Greg And I'll try Chinese food some other time—when I'm on my own!

2 Write E (Emily), J (Juan), or G (Greg).

1 .... suggests going to Leo's.
2 .... likes baked potatoes with sour cream.
3 .... doesn't want to go to the same place again.
4 .... wants to try Chinese food for the first time.
5 .... isn't sure Greg will like Chinese food.
6 .... says she will pay for lunch.

Get talking Making offers

40

3 Complete the dialogues using words from the box. There are two you won't use. Then listen and check.

make a picnic   do your homework   pay   get the phone   buy a new coat

A Let's go to Leo's Burger Bar.
B Great. I'll ¹........................

A Let's go to the beach.
B That's a good idea. I'll ²....................

A Let's call for pizza.
B OK. I'll ³....................

4 Match the actions and the pictures.

1 buy flowers   3 wash the car   5 close the curtains
2 eat a sandwich   4 turn on the TV   6 open the window

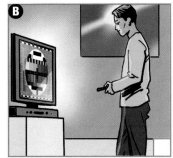

5 Work with a partner. Use the dialogues from Exercise 3 and the prompts below to make mini-dialogues.

1 go for a bike ride tomorrow   4 get something to eat
2 get some air in this room   5 get Julia a thank-you present
3 watch the game   6 watch the movie in the dark

Language Focus

Vocabulary Food

 41 **1** Write the correct number on the left. Then listen and check.

	broiled fish
	raw carrot
	baked potato
	roasted chicken
	grilled cheese
	fried egg

 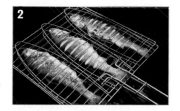 

 42 **2** Match the questions and answers. Listen and check.

1 How do you like eggs?   a) I like them raw.
2 How do you like potatoes?   b) I don't. I'm a vegetarian.
3 How do you like carrots?   c) I like them fried with ketchup.
4 How do you like chicken?   d) I like them scrambled.

Get talking Talking about food

3 Work with a partner. Ask the questions from Exercise 2. Talk about other foods.

4 Complete using the words on the left.

hot
rich
sweet
sour
~~mild~~
light

Salsa can be
mild. or
..............!

Apples can be
.... or
..............!

Chocolate cake can be
.... or
..............!

Grammar

Will / won't Predictions

1 **Complete the sentences from page 64 with *'ll* or *won't*.**

1 There .... be a lot of things on the menu that aren't too hot.
2 If I'm with you, it .... be great!
3 I'm not sure you .... like it.
4 You .... regret it, Em.
5 I .... pay for the meal.

2 **Complete the rule with *will* and *won't*.**

When we are sure about something in the future, we can use *will* (*'ll*) or [1]..................... (= *will not*) plus the infinitive of the verb. In speaking, [2]..................... is often shortened to *'ll*.

3 **Complete the sentences with the correct verb from the box.**

will be	won't be	will have	won't have

1 Fifty people are coming to the party? That's too many. There .... enough food.
2 Next Monday is a holiday, so we .... any classes.
3 Hurry up, or we .... late!
4 Let's walk to school. The bus .... a long time.
5 I'm so thirsty. I think I .... some water.
6 We can't visit James tomorrow. We .... enough time.

4 **Complete Student B's replies with *'ll* or *won't*.**

1 **A** I'm going to try eating raw steak.
  B Really? I don't think you .... like it.
2 **A** I don't know how to make a stir-fry.
  B Ask Jeff to come over. He .... show you.
3 **A** I feel like a pizza.
  B OK, let's go to La Fornia, I'm sure you .... love their pizza!
4 **A** I invited Julie to the barbecue tomorrow.
  B Well, she hates meat, so I'm sure she .... come.
5 **A** Don't put salt in the soup.
  B But if I don't, it .... taste horrible.
6 **A** I eat tons of fast food. I love it.
  B Well, you .... be sorry when you're older!

Question tags (review)

5 **Complete the question tags. Look at the dialogue on page 64 to check your answers.**

1 He doesn't have to order something hot, ... he?
2 There's no point in going, ... there?
3 He said he wants to try Chinese food, ... he?

6 **Circle the correct question tag.**

1 It's easy, (*isn't it*)/ *doesn't it*?
2 The movie was really bad, *wasn't it / didn't it*?
3 We aren't late, *aren't we / are we*?
4 She lives in that house, *isn't it / doesn't she*?
5 You like salsa, *don't you / do you*?
6 You're going to be there, *don't you / aren't you*?
7 It won't rain tomorrow, *is it / will it*?
8 You know where he lives, *don't you / doesn't he*?

7 **Complete the question tags.**

1 She's French, ... she?
2 These apples are delicious, ... they?
3 You don't know the answer, ... you?
4 Japanese people love good food, ... they?

5 The meal wasn't very expensive, ... it?
6 You've never eaten Italian food, ... you?
7 They didn't like it, ... they?
8 You went to Florida last year, ... you?

8 **Complete the sentences with a question tag.**

1 You're Australian, ...?

2 You don't know how to get to the mall, ...?

3 We're in the wrong place, ...?

4 The beans are pretty spicy, ...?

5 You know a lot about animals, ...?

6 You aren't a very good dancer, ...?

Skills

Reading

1 Read the text and answer the questions

1 What does Jamie Oliver do?
2 Which city did Jamie want to make an example of?
3 What does *Food Revolution* do?

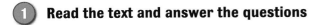

Food Revolution

Jamie Oliver is a world-famous English chef who owns and runs his own restaurants, and trains new chefs. He also hosts TV shows about how to eat healthier and better food.

In March 2010, a new TV show called *Food Revolution* premiered in the U.S. The show takes a look at health problems caused by unhealthy eating habits.

In the show, Jamie visits Huntington, West Virginia. It was named the "unhealthiest city in America." Jamie wants to make Huntington healthy again. By doing so, he hopes to inspire other communities to change the way they eat for the better.

Jamie believes that everyone has a "right" to healthy food. With the show, he hopes to make people aware of the foods that are bad for them.

2 Here are some facts and figures about obesity in the U.S. Match the headings with the correct text.

1 Childhood obesity   3 Diabetes
2 Obesity in West Virginia   4 Too sweet

A ☐

About 27 percent of Americans are classified as obese, and that number is growing. One major contributor to obesity in the U.S. is sugar. Sugar is added to many food products such as soft drinks, ice cream, and sugary snacks. Teenage boys eat an average of 34 teaspoons of added sugar each day. That's more than three times the recommended amount of 10 teaspoons for each American.

B ☐

Nearly one in three American children are overweight or obese. Most obese children—about 80 percent of them—will also be obese as adults. Children in the U.S. are predicted to be the first generation to die before their parents. This is due to obesity-related health problems.

C ☐

About eight percent of the U.S. population has diabetes. About 90 percent of those with diabetes have type 2 diabetes. Much of this is caused by obesity. Type 2 diabetes is increasingly being found in teenagers and children.

D ☐

West Virginia has the third-highest level of adult obesity in the U.S. More than 31 percent of people living there are obese. More than 35 percent of teenagers are overweight or obese. More people in West Virginia have diabetes than in any other state.

3 Read the texts again. Answer the questions.

1 What is one big reason why people become obese?
2 Why do experts think some children will die before their parents?
3 What is a major cause of Type 2 diabetes?
4 What percentage of people are obese in West Virginia?

Speaking

4 Match each word with its definition.

1	artificial	a)	has good effects on your body
2	harmful	b)	makes you become heavier
3	healthy	c)	full of the natural things your body needs
4	nutritious	d)	not natural; manufactured
5	fresh	e)	tastes good
6	tasty	f)	makes you feel full or that you have eaten a lot of food
7	disgusting	g)	new; not frozen or in a can
8	filling	h)	has bad effects; doesn't do you good
9	fattening	i)	tastes very bad

5 Look at the food below. Write the names.

1 s.................... 2 o.................... 3 m.................... 4 b.................... 5 y.................... 6 h....................

7 c.................... 8 c.................... 9 p.................... 10 h.................... 11 c.................... 12 c....................

6 Work with a partner. Describe the foods from Exercise 5.

I think yogurt is …

I hate …! I think it's disgusting.

Yes, but it's ….

Listening

7 **Listen to the radio show. Number the cities in order of how healthy they are (1 = most healthy → 5 = least healthy).**

Denver, Colorado

San Jose, California

New York City, New York

New Orleans, Louisiana

Seattle, Washington

8 **Listen again. Correct each sentence.**

1   Cities in the eastern U.S. are healthier than those in the west.
2   California has five of the top five healthiest cities.
3   Denver, Colorado was number 10.
4   New Yorkers live in one of the most healthy cities in the U.S.

Writing for your Portfolio

9 **Read the text. Do you think Paul has a healthy diet? Give reasons.**

I often miss breakfast. I'm not very hungry in the morning. But I usually take some fresh fruit with me to school, like an apple or banana that I can eat between classes. I have lunch at school, usually something with french fries, like a hamburger or some chicken nuggets. Not very nutritious, I know. When I get home in the afternoon, my mom makes me a grilled cheese sandwich or something. In the evening, we usually all have dinner at different times. I have something like a hotdog and potato chips, but sometimes I'll eat spaghetti and meatballs.

10 **Write a short text about what you eat.**

Sounds right Question intonation

11 **Look back at the questions in Exercise 8 on page 68. Practice saying the questions as if you already know the answer (giving an opinion with a falling tone at the end) and then as a real check question (with a rising tone at the end). Then test your partner.**

Musical styles

Key words

performer	emerge	movement	breakdancing
producer	moody	graffiti	decline

1 **Read the texts. Which of these musical styles do you know about/like?**

One of the most popular movies from the late 1970s was *Saturday Night Fever*. It told the story of a young dancer played by John Travolta and showed that disco music was big business. Disco had first started a few years earlier with performers such as Donna Summer, The Bee Gees, and Sister Sledge. However, the real stars were the producers of the records who often wrote and created the songs. By the end of the decade, "disco" was popular all over the world. It started to decline in popularity in the early 1980s.

Teen pop is a style of music geared toward teenagers, but it can include all kinds of music genres—pop, dance, hip-hop, rock, etc. Teen pop first became popular in the 1980s and then died down in the late 1990s. But in the 2000s, teen pop had a major revival, thanks in part to movies such as *High School Musical* and *School of Rock* and TV shows such as *Hannah Montana* and *Camp Rock*. Many teen stars have met with great success during the past decade, including Miley Cyrus and the Jonas Brothers.

If one album defines early-1990s rock music, then it has to be Nirvana's *Nevermind*. Suddenly music magazines all over the world were writing about a new sound that was coming from the American city of Seattle—grunge. Grunge is a style of alternative music influenced by punk, heavy metal, and indie rock. The music is often dark and moody. It became very popular with many teenagers who felt it illustrated their lives. Now grunge has lost a lot of its popularity, but many of the original bands, such as Pearl Jam, Mudhoney, and Alice in Chains, continue to attract new teenage audiences.

During the mid-1970s, a new style of music started in the black neighborhoods of American cities. It was known as hip-hop. By 1979 it had become very successful, and songs such as *Rapper's Delight* by The Sugarhill Gang were big in many countries. Hip-hop music consists of two parts; DJing (producing and scratching) and rapping (speaking along to the music). However, hip-hop is not just about music—breakdancing and graffiti are also important parts of the culture. These days hip-hop is still popular, and artists such as Eminem and Kanye West enjoy huge success all over the world.

2 **Work in groups. What kind of music do you think these musicians play?**

punk   the blues   pop   heavy metal   techno   country

3 **Listen to the extracts of songs. Which style of music are they?**

1 ....
2 ....
3 ....
4 ....
5 ....
6 ....

Discuss with your group:

- what the music sounds like
- where it came/comes from
- when it was popular
- some of the performers associated with it

Mini-project Battle of the bands

4 **Research your favorite band and write a report about them.**

Include:
- what style of music they play
- a note on similar bands
- a look at some of the bands who influenced them
- some photographs

5 **Present your report in class and play an example of some of their music.**

1 Read the texts and match with the photos.
(Be careful, one text doesn't have a photo!)

In this unit

You learn

- could, might, may for speculation
- -ed vs. -ing adjectives
- words for body movements

and then you can

- talk about emotions
- talk about body movements

A
If you show the soles of your feet or shoes in Thailand, people could find it insulting. The soles are the lowest part of the body, so people think they are "dirty."

B
Do you smile when you want to greet someone in a friendly way? In some cultures people don't smile in this situation, and in others people smile for different reasons. Some Japanese people, for example, may smile when they are confused or angry.

C
In the Middle East and Far East, it is not polite to point with your index finger. You should only point with an open hand (or your thumb in Indonesia), never with your index finger.

D
Every culture has a "comfort zone" for personal space when people talk to one another. For Western Europeans and Americans, a distance between people of 35–50 cm is comfortable. In Japan, people prefer more space, about 90 cm. People in the Middle East may feel strange if the person they're talking to is so far away, though, since they prefer shorter distances of 20–25 cm.

E
You might find it interesting to know that in the Middle East and Far East, you should never pass something to another person with your left hand. People think the left hand is "unclean." In Japan, you should use both hands.

F
Do you think nodding your head up and down means "yes" all over the world? You might be surprised if you went to Greece or Bulgaria. In those countries, nodding means "No!"

2 **Write the name of the correct country.**

In which country (or region)...
1 should you use your thumb to point?   ....
2 do people think the bottom of the foot is not clean?   ....
3 might people smile if they don't understand something?   ....
4 should you always use two hands to give someone something? ....
5 should you not get much closer than one meter to someone?   ....
6 could a "yes" be mistaken for a "no?"   ....

Get talking Talking about emotions

3 **Match the emotions to the correct picture.**

disappointed   frightened   bored   tired   excited   interested

2

4 **Listen and repeat.**

A I didn't really like the talk. I thought it was boring.
B Really? I wasn't bored at all.

A I thought the football game was really exciting.
B Really? I didn't find it exciting at all.

5 **Work with a partner. Use the prompts to make similar dialogues.**

1 horror movie /
   frightening

2 documentary /
   interesting

3 book / disappointing

4 walk / tiring

Language Focus

Vocabulary Body movements

1 **Match the gestures to the pictures.**

> 1 fold your arms 2 cross your legs 3 nod your head 4 scratch your head
> 5 shake your head 6 wave 7 point a finger 8 shake hands

Get talking Talking about body movements

2 **Complete the sentences.**

1 I usually f............................ my arms when I'm angry with someone.
2 I always c............................ my legs when I sit.
3 I always w............................ when I say goodbye to my mom in the mornings.
4 I never p............................ because I think it's rude.
5 I always s............................ hands when I meet a new person.
6 I s............................ my head when I don't want something.
7 I sometimes n............................ my head when I agree with someone.
8 I only s............................ my head when I think.

3 **Work with a partner. Are these sentences true for you? Say if they are different.**

> I fold my arms when I'm waiting.

> I don't think pointing is rude.

> I usually kiss on the cheek when I meet a new person.

Grammar

Could, might, may for speculation

1 **Look at the examples from the texts on page 74.**

1 If you show the soles of your feet or shoes in Thailand, people **could** find it insulting.
2 You **might** be surprised if you went to Greece or Bulgaria.
3 Some Japanese people, for example, **may** smile when they are confused or angry.

Rule
We can use *could*, *might*, and *may* to talk about possible situations and hypothesize about a situation. We also use *will* (it's definite that) and *won't* (it's definitely not). As always, these modal verbs are followed by the infinitive without *to*.

2 **Complete the sentences using the words on the right.**

1 He's speaking Spanish, so he .... from Argentina.
2 Look at the sky. It .... later.
3 They're not playing very well. I think they .... if they're not careful.
4 It's a difficult exam, but she .... if she studies really hard.
5 Look in the kitchen. You .... your keys there.
6 I'm so tired I .... asleep in the middle of the movie.

could be
could pass
might find
might fall
might rain
may lose

3 **Look at the photos. Which parts of the body are they? Choose from the words on the right and write sentences.**

  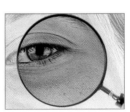 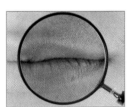

1 *It could be hair.* 2 .... 3 .... 4 ....
....

 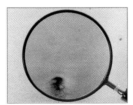  

5 .... 6 .... 7 .... 8 ....
....

mouth
ear
stomach
hair
throat
finger
eye
foot

4 **Rewrite the sentences using the words in parentheses.**

1 Ask Joe. It's possible he knows the answer. (may) ....
2 I'm not sure. It's possibly a problem with your Internet provider. (might) ....
3 She's very upset. It's possible she'll start crying. (may) ....
4 That wall looks very unsafe. It's possible it'll fall down anytime. (could) ....

-ed vs. -ing adjectives

(5) **Look at the examples from the texts on page 74 and underline the adjectives.**

1 .... people could find it insulting.
2 Some Japanese people, for example, may smile when they are confused.
3 You might find it interesting to know...
4 You might be surprised if you went to Greece or Bulgaria.

Rule

Some adjectives have two forms; *bored/boring, confused/confusing, surprised/surprising,* etc.
Generally we use the **-ed** adjective to describe the feeling we have.
I'm tired (I want to sleep)
We use the **-ing** adjective to describe the things that produce that feeling.
The walk was tiring (it made me tired)

(6) **Write the sentences on the right under the correct picture.**

1 .... 2 .... 3 ....

4 .... 5 .... 6 ....

He's bored.
It's amazing.
It's frightening.
He's frightened.
He's amazed.
He's boring.

(7) **Complete the sentences using the words on the right.**

1 It's 6:00 p.m. and Dave still isn't home. I'm a little ....
2 All I got were some socks for my birthday. It was so ....
3 I don't like the way you are talking to me. I find it ....
4 If you're so ...., why don't you go to bed?
5 I met Alex Rodriguez! It was the most .... day of my life. He's so great.
6 I don't want to go to the auto museum. I'm not really .... in old cars.

worried
insulting
disappointing
interested
exciting
tired

(8) **Circle the correct word.**

1 I hate football. I find it so *bored / boring.*
2 No one came to my party. I was so *disappointed / disappointing.*
3 I still get really *excited / exciting* at Christmas.
4 Have you read this article about nano-technology? It's *fascinated / fascinating.*
5 I didn't sleep well at all last night. I'm so *tired / tiring* today.
6 I've got an important exam tomorrow and I'm a little *worried / worrying* about it.
7 I can't find my phone. It's kind of *worried / worrying.*
8 Here's your present. I hope you're not *disappointed / disappointing* by it.

Skills

Reading

1. **Read the text. Who lived longer ago, Ötzi or Sir Walter Ralegh?**

A short *history* *of* *piercing*

The trendy ice man

What does Ötzi (the name for the mummy found a few years ago near the Austrian-Italian border) have in common with people who want to be trendy? Body piercing! The "ice man" from about 4,000 years ago had pierced ears!

Piercing in the ancient world

In the ancient world, body piercing was often a symbol of courage and class. That's why it was popular with the pharaohs in Egypt and with important people in ancient Rome. Tongue piercing was part of a religious ritual of the high priests of the Aztecs. They believed that if their tongues were pierced, they could communicate better with the gods.

Piercing in Africa and Central America

In some areas of these continents, people believed that demons could enter the body through the ears. So they pierced their ears and put ornaments in. They thought that the metal would stop demons from getting into the body.

Piercing in Elizabethan England

In England in the late 1500s, famous men such as Shakespeare, Sir Walter Ralegh, and Francis Drake wore gold rings in their ears. In those days, sailors also wore earrings, for two reasons: firstly, they thought they could see better if their ears were pierced; and secondly, they thought, "If our ship sinks and we die, and our bodies are found on the beach, the gold earrings will pay for our funeral."

Piercing today

In the United States in the 1980s, body piercing increasingly became a form of rebellion for young people. Later, it lost its rebellious meaning and just became fashionable. Because

more and more movie stars and athletes were getting pierced, young people wanted to imitate them.

2. **Read the text again and complete the table.**

Who?	Where?	Why?
Ötzi	ears	reason not given
Aztec priests		
Africans		
Elizabethan sailors		
Young Americans in the 1980s		

Listening and speaking

3 *Fantastic Voyage* is a cult movie from 1966. Listen to the story and find two mistakes in the picture.

4 Listen again. Match the sentence halves to make a summary of the story.

1 *Fantastic Voyage* is set
2 An important scientist is
3 The voyage is
4 A miniature submarine travels
5 The submarine has
6 This crew includes
7 The mission can't
8 One of the crew may be

a) dying from a blood clot.
b) in the bloodstream to reach his brain.
c) trying to destroy the mission.
d) a journey inside his body.
e) a crew of five people.
f) a pilot, a doctor, and his assistant, a bloodstream expert, and an agent.
g) during the Cold War.
h) take longer than an hour.

5 Work in groups. Discuss the questions and make up your own ending to the story. Then tell your stories to the rest of the class and vote on the best one.

1 How does the submarine get into the body?
2 What obstacles do they meet inside the body?
3 Who is trying to destroy the mission and why?
4 How do they discover who it is?
5 How do they break up the clot?
6 Do they get out in time?
7 Is the mission a success?
8 What happens due to this mission?

6 Read the DVD review of *Fantastic Voyage*. Check the things that the critic likes.

☐ the story   ☐ the special effects   ☐ the actors
☐ the music   ☐ the dialogue

Classic DVDs

Fantastic Voyage is a great adventure movie for the whole family, and it is as entertaining today as it was 40 years ago. It's true that the special effects are a little out-of-date, but that helps give the movie its appeal. The story is great. It involves a mission inside the human body to save the life of a scientist who can save the world. It's exciting and keeps you watching until the very end of the movie. It also stars some of the great screen icons of the 1960s, including Raquel Welch, Stephen Boyd, and Donald Pleasence. Highly recommended.

Writing for your Portfolio

7 Write a mini-review of an old movie you have seen.

Check your progress Units 7 and 8

1 Complete the words.

1 r _ _ eggs/meat/vegetables
2 f _ _ _ _ potatoes/chicken/eggs
3 b _ _ _ _ _ vegetables
4 g _ _ _ _ _ _ cheese sandwich
5 r _ _ _ _ chicken

6 f _ _ _ your arms
7 c _ _ _ _ your legs
8 n _ _ or s _ _ _ _ _ _ your head
9 s _ _ _ _ hands / your head   ☐ 10

2 Write sentences with the correct adjective.

1 She / interest / in movies

....

2 He / very insult / to her

....

3 It's a / fright / DVD

....

4 They / worry / about their exams

....

5 It's a / disappoint / result

....

6 The instructions are / confuse

....
                                                   ☐ 12

3 Complete the dialogue with the correct question tag or adjective.

A I'm really ¹.................. (boring). There's nothing to do!

B It's three thirty, ².................. ? There's a space documentary on TV.

A Let's watch it! You like space shows, ³.................. ?

B Yes, I love them. They're ⁴.................. (fascinate).

A You have a lot of books about space, ⁵.................. ?

B I don't, but my brother does. But, yes, space is ⁶.................. (amaze)!   ☐ 6

4 Write the question tags.

1 John isn't coming to your party, ...
2 It was Karen who bought the flowers, ...
3 John and David aren't brothers, ...
4 Jeannette goes to school with you, ...
5 We don't have to tell anyone, ...
6 You won't forget, ...   ☐ 6

5 Write sentences using *could, may,* or *might*. Use the words in parentheses.

1 Don't speak like that. You will insult people.
  If you ....
  (be insulted)

2 People in Japan may stand farther away from each other than people in the U.S.
  People in Japan ....
  (uncomfortable / stand too close)

3 He's speaking French. Maybe he's from France.
  He's speaking ....
  (so he)

4 The sky is black. There's a chance that it will rain later.
  The sky .... (so it)

5 You need to study more or you will fail your exam.
  If you don't ....
  (fail)

6 I think there is more information about this on the Internet.
  You ....
  (find)

7 Perhaps this piece of metal is from an old car.
  This .... (be from)

8 Take it back to the store. Maybe they will give you your money back.
  They ....
  (if you ask)   ☐ 16

    TOTAL ☐ 50

My progress so far is ...

☺   😐   ☹

great! ☐   good. ☐   poor. ☐

Street performers!

1 **Read about a festival in Canada and answer the questions.**

Street performers and street musicians have been around since ancient times. Until there was recorded music, most entertainers made money by performing in this way. The actor Robin Williams and the rock star Eric Clapton both started their careers as street performers!

The Edmonton International Street Performers' Festival is Canada's oldest street theater festival. It has been held since 1983 in the city of Edmonton. Every year, more than 50 of the world's best street performers take part in the festival.

During the festival, you can watch comedians, actors, clowns, musicians, and masked characters walk around the festival site and entertain their audience. All the entertainment is free.

In the first year of the festival, there was a performer called Philippe Petit, a French high-wire artist. This daring man became famous in 1974 when he illegally put a wire between the World Trade Center Towers and walked across it, 400 meters above the streets of New York City. In Canada, he walked from the fifth floor of one building to the eleventh floor of another.

Apart from street entertainment, there is another side to the festival. As part of the Comedy Cares program, performers use their amazing talents in local hospitals to make patients, family, and staff laugh.

1 Where is Edmonton?
2 Who takes part in the Edmonton festival?
3 How much does it cost to see each performance?
4 Where did Philippe Petit perform his most daring high-wire walk?
5 Where is the Comedy Cares program performed?

5 **2** **Listen to the interview with Karen, a human statue. Then circle T (True) or F (False).**

1 You shouldn't scare anyone. T / F
2 Design your costume to look like a statue you see in a park or museum. T / F
3 Choose a dark-brown or green color for your makeup and costume. T / F
4 Stand on something so that you are taller than the crowd. T / F
5 Learn to move slowly like a robot. T / F

3 **Over 2 U!** **In groups, design a human statue for your town. Answer these questions.**

Where will the statue stand? What will it look like? What will you use to make the costume? What will the statue do to entertain people?

 **Now you can watch Episode 4 of *School Reporters!***

It must be her age

When Mom and I came into the living room, Aunt Nancy sighed and Uncle Jack looked at me and shouted, "Look, it's Dracula's daughter!" And then he laughed like crazy. I ignored them and walked across their ugly orange carpet to the sofa. From there I could see myself in the mirror.

I looked cool. I looked Goth. Black clothes, fishnet tights, heavy boots. White face, black eyeliner, black lipstick. Totally, totally Goth. They all looked at me. Mom said, "It's her age, you know. It's a phase." Aunt Nancy smiled sadly and Uncle Jack said, "Does it speak?" "Ha-ha!" I said. "Yes, I can hear and speak." "Good," he said, "because with all that black stuff around your eyes, you probably can't see." He looked at Mom and his wife for some applause, and they both giggled.

"I hope she doesn't look like that on the wedding day," Aunt Nancy said. "Joy wouldn't want her to look like that." "Oh no," Mom said quickly. "She'll wear the dress Joy bought for her. Won't you, Felicity?" "Mom, please!" I said. "Sorry, Flicka. That's what she likes to be called

Goth

now", Mom said to Aunt Nancy. "And what's that on its neck?" Uncle Jack shouted. "A tattoo," I said. "A tattoo of a spider's web." "Not a real one!" Mom said, hastily again. "It's a wash-off one." "Wash-off, eh?" my uncle said.

I ignored him. I was embarrassed. I would have liked a real tattoo and not my wash-off one. I didn't say anything for the rest of the evening.

The dress Joy gave me was horrible. All pastels and white and cute. But I've always liked my cousin Joy. "I know I'm asking a lot, but I really want you to wear it for the wedding," Joy said. "You're my bridesmaid and I want everything to be just right."

On the day of the wedding, I felt terrible. But Joy looked really happy, so I tried to smile, too. Everyone was wearing suits and flowery dresses. Yuck. And then I saw a cute boy. He had a suit and short hair, but he didn't look bad. Not bad at all. A few minutes later he walked over to me. "Cousin of the bride?" he said. "Yes," I said. "And who are you?" "I'm Lawrence. Cousin of the bridegroom."

For **MORE!** Go to www.cambridge.org/elt/americanmore and take a quiz on this text.

UNIT 9 Fame

1 Listen and read.

Greg I think I'll stay home tonight. Is there anything worth watching on TV?

Emily Of course! The Grammys are on!

Greg The what?

Juan The Grammys. It's an award ceremony. They're awards for musicians.

Greg You mean like the Academy Awards but for music? I used to watch the Oscars on TV in Brazil.

Juan Oh? So, you're into watching award shows? Well, I'm sure you'll enjoy the Grammys, too.

Emily So who do you think's going to win, Juan?

Juan I don't know. I'm not very good at predicting things. But Beyoncé might get best female vocalist.

Emily No way. Taylor Swift will definitely win that.

Greg Who is she?

Emily Taylor Swift? She's really famous. Do you know that song, "You Belong With Me?"

Greg Oh, yeah, I know that one. But I didn't know it was Taylor Swift.

Emily So, Juan, can I borrow your MP3 player?

Juan What's wrong with yours?

Emily I left it at home. And I need to give Greg a lesson in good music.

Juan Here you go. But I don't have Taylor Swift on it anymore. I took her album off.

Emily What?

Juan Yeah, that's right. I mean, I used to like Taylor Swift. But she's so overplayed now. I'm kind of sick of hearing it.

Greg So who do you like these days?

Juan Stuff like Kanye West and Beyoncé.

Greg Now *that's* what I call good music!

2 **Circle the correct word.**

1 The Grammy awards are for *musicians / actors*.
2 The Grammys are *a British / an American* award ceremony.
3 Juan thinks *Beyoncé / Taylor Swift* might win the best female vocalist award.
4 "You Belong With Me" is a song by *Beyoncé / Taylor Swift*.
5 *Emily / Juan* left *her / his* MP3 player at home.
6 Emily wants to tell Greg about *an MP3 player / good music*.
7 Juan *has never liked Taylor Swift / liked Taylor Swift in the past*.
8 Greg *likes / doesn't like* Kanye West.

Get talking Talking about past and present favorites

3 **Put the dialogues in the correct order. Then listen and check.**

A ...... Don't you like Black Eyed Peas anymore?
..1.. Who's your favorite band?
...... I used to like them, but now I prefer Kings of Leon.
...... I think it's Kings of Leon.

B ...... Don't you like Brad Pitt anymore?
...... I think it's Vince Vaughan.
...... I used to like him, but now I prefer Vince Vaughan.
...... Who's your favorite actor?

C ...... I used to like that, but now I prefer watching TV.
...... What's your favorite pastime?
...... Don't you like playing computer games anymore?
...... I think it's watching TV.

4 **Complete the chart.**

	In the past	Now
My favorite actress		
My favorite singer		
My favorite pastime		
My favorite weekend activity		

5 **Work with a partner. Use the chart and make similar dialogues to Exercise 3.**

Language Focus

Vocabulary Award shows

1 Look at the words below. Say if they describe an award ceremony, movies, or music.

> solo male artist   picture   actress   solo female artist
> group   album   animated movie   actor   single

Get talking Talking about awards

2 Which awards in Exercise 1 could these people or movies win?

A Akon

B *Spiderman III*

C Angelina Jolie

D Beyoncé

E The Rolling Stones

F *Ta-Dah* by the Scissor Sisters

G *Cars*

H Brad Pitt

I "Crazy" by Gnarls Barkley

> **A** Akon. Is he an actor?

> **B** No, he's a singer. He could win best solo male artist.

3 Listen and check your answers.

4 Work in groups of four. You are going to give the award in each of the categories above.

> **A** And my winner for this category is Angelina Jolie.

> **B** And the winner for the best solo male artist of last year is Akon.

Grammar

Used to (review)

1 **Look at the example sentences from page 84 and answer the questions.**

I **used to watch** the Oscars on TV in Brazil. (Greg)
I **used to like** Taylor Swift. (Juan)

1 Does Greg still watch the Oscars?
2 Does Juan still like Taylor Swift?

To talk about past habits, we can use *used to* + the infinitive.
I **used to** love *Sesame Street*.
I **didn't use to** watch any TV.
Did you **use to** watch a lot of TV?

2 **Write sentences about Josh.**

1 *He used to play piano, but now he plays guitar.*

2 ....

3 ....

4 ....

5 ....

6 ....

3 **Put the words in order.**

1 Jersey / I / to / live / used / New / in ....
2 school / I / didn't / to / like / use ....
3 star / to / used / a / she / movie / be ....
4 me / use / they / to / like / didn't ....
5 same / she / to / as / go / you /
   did / to / the / use / school? ....

4 **Work with a partner. Ask and answer questions.**

When you were seven, did you use to:
1 watch cartoons?
2 walk to school on your own?
3 like vegetables?
4 share a bedroom?

A Yes, I did and I still do.

B No, I didn't.

Gerunds after prepositions

5 **Match the beginnings and endings.**

1 Greg is thinking of …	watching award shows.
2 He's into …	predicting things.
3 Juan's not very good at …	staying in.

6 **Circle the correct options to complete the rule.**

Many verbs and adjectives are followed by *an adjective / a preposition*. If we want to use a verb after the preposition, the verb is in the *infinitive / -ing* form.

7 **Complete the sentences using phrases from the box.**

on going	of sitting	on playing	in buying	to going	at reading

1 Jane was planning .... parachute jumping.

2 They were interested .... a bigger car.

3 Brian was terrible .... maps.

4 He's a big fan .... in the sun.

5 She's looking forward .... to Arizona tomorrow.

6 She insisted .... the violin.

8 **Complete each sentence with the correct preposition and form of the verb in parentheses.**

1 My brother's good .... models. (make)
2 I'm no good .... computers. (use)
3 My friends are thinking .... a party next weekend. (have)
4 My uncle's coming next week. I'm looking forward .... him again. (see)
5 I've never really been interested .... to other countries. (travel)
6 It was very boring, but he insisted .... me the whole story. (tell)
7 My parents are planning .... to Peru for their next vacation. (go)
8 I don't like playing football very much, but I'm really .... it. (watch)

Skills

Reading

1 Read the article. Write the paragraph headings in the correct places.

> The law   Charity work   Money

Famous... *but are they happy?*

Wouldn't we all like to be famous? With a lot of money, freedom, power and respect? And fans – people who love you. But many famous people are not very happy. Why is that?

A ....

When you become famous, many things change in your life. Usually, you get rich. And sometimes very rich people do strange things with their money.

In November 2000, Elton John was asked in a British court if it was true that he had spent a lot of money on flowers between January 1996 and September 1997. John replied: "Yes, I like flowers." How much did he spend? About $430,000!

B ....

Sometimes we think that famous people have more freedom than ordinary people. That's not really true, but there are some famous people who think the law is not for them.

A lot of stars forget that they cannot just do whatever they want. Winona Ryder learned that lesson. She tried to steal expensive designer clothes from a store in Beverly Hills. Her crime was reported in newspapers and on TV news shows. Now she isn't as successful as she used to be.

C ....

Some stars use their fame in a positive way, because they understand that they can use their power to make the world a better place. Take the example of movie star Angelina Jolie. When she was making a movie in Cambodia, she met a lot of people who had to leave their homes. Now Angelina does charity work in several countries, meeting and helping as many people as she can.

2 Read the text again and decide if the sentences are **T (True)** or **F (False)**.

1 Elton John spent about $430,000 on flowers in one year. T / F
2 Winona Ryder tried to steal expensive clothes. T / F
3 Angelina Jolie saw a movie about poor people in Cambodia. T / F
4 Angelina Jolie does charity work in seven countries. T / F

Listening

9 **3** **Listen to Greg talking about famous people. Circle the correct answers.**

1 Greg The person I want to meet most is ...

Shakira   Madonna   Jennifer Lopez

because:

a) I'm a fan of her music.
b) I think she's a great person.
c) she has done a lot for other people.
d) she's beautiful.

2 The two questions I want to ask her are:

a) Where do you get the ideas for your songs?
b) What was life like for you when you were a teenager?
c) Have you ever been poor?
d) Do you like being famous?

10 **4** **Now listen to Annie. Complete the notes.**

Barack Obama   Steven Spielberg   Bill Gates

Annie The person I want to meet most is ....
because ....

The two questions I want to ask him are:
1 ....
2 ....

Writing for your Portfolio

5 **Read the profile of Shaun White.**

All about Shaun White
- He is a professional snowboarder and skateboarder.
- He was born on September 3, 1986, in San Diego, California.
- Shaun started snowboarding when he was six.
- He has won a lot of gold medals in the X Games.
- He has won two Olympic gold medals.
- His fans call him the "flying tomato" because he has long red hair.

6 **Think of a famous person you admire. Write a profile similar to the one above.**

A Song 4 U Fame

11 (7) **Listen and sing. Put a check next to the things mentioned in the song.**

1 Fame is free. ☐
2 Fame lives forever. ☐
3 Fame is easily forgotten. ☐
4 Fame lights up the sky. ☐
5 Fame makes people love you. ☐
6 Fame can catch the moon. ☐
7 Fame can break your heart. ☐
8 Fame is tough. ☐

Reading and writing

(8) **Now read the text about Shaun. What information from the profile in Exercise 5 has been taken out? What extra information has been included?**

A famous person that I really admire is the professional snowboarder and skateboarder Shaun White. Shaun was born in San Diego, California, on September 3, 1986, and by the age of six he was already snowboarding. He started competing when he was 13 and turned professional when he was 17. Although he is still very young, he has already won many gold medals in the X Games.

He has won two Olympic gold medals. I'm sure he will win many more. I'm a big fan of Shaun's because I love extreme sports and he shows us the kinds of things a young person can achieve.

(9) **Now turn your profile from Exercise 6 into a short text.**

Sounds right Questions

(10) **Questions you might want to use for interviews with famous people beginning with Wh-words (*when, where, what*) often have the following stress pattern: OooO. Write three more questions and practice saying them.**

O	o	o	o	o	o	o	o	O
Where	do	you	get	the	ideas	for	your	songs?
What	was	life	like	for	you	as	a	teenager?

The city of Vancouver

Learn MORE through English

Key words

quality of life	current	community	climate
rainfall	scenery	temperate	minority

1 **Read the text. Would you like to go to Vancouver? Why or why not?**

Vancouver is a city in the southwest of British Columbia, very close to the border with the U.S. It is the third largest city in Canada (after Toronto and Montreal). The population of Greater Vancouver is just over 2 million people. It is named after a British explorer, Captain George Vancouver.

Vancouver is notable for several things. It is the third largest film production center in North America (after Los Angeles and New York City). It is also a city with a good quality of life. In 2007, Vancouver was equal to Vienna as having the third-highest quality of living in the world, after Zurich and Geneva.

It is a popular place for tourists, too, due mostly to its geography. Vancouver is set on the coast between the Strait of Georgia and the North Shore Mountains.

The city is famous for its beautiful scenery, and it has one of the largest city parks in North America, called Stanley Park. The North Shore Mountains can be seen from many places within the city, and on a clear day the views include Mount Baker (a snow-capped volcano in the state of Washington) to the southeast, Vancouver Island across the Strait of Georgia to the west and southwest, and the Sunshine Coast to the northwest. Vancouver also has beaches that are popular with residents and tourists during the summer. The mountains also offer skiing (nearby Whistler hosted the Winter Olympic Games in 2010).

Vancouver's climate is very temperate by Canadian standards, due to the warm ocean current that flows past the city. The summer months are sunny and temperatures are moderate (the daily maximum averages 22°C in July and August) and are often fairly dry. In contrast, more than half of all winter days receive measurable rainfall. On average, snow falls on only 11 days per year, with only three days receiving six centimeters or more.

2 **Take the quiz.**

1 What are the two official languages of Canada?
   a) English and French   b) English and Spanish   c) English and Chinese
2 Which two languages are most spoken in Vancouver?
   a) English and French   b) English and Spanish   c) English and Chinese
3 What percentage of Vancouver's population is white?
   a) 51%   b) 71%   c) 75%
4 What are the two largest minority groups in Vancouver?
   a) Chinese and French   b) Chinese and Indian   c) Indian and Vietnamese

3 **Read the text and check your answers.**

Hongcouver

Many people know that Canada has two official languages, which are English and French. This is why the information on anything you buy in Canada is written in both languages. But not many people know that in Vancouver, the two main languages you'll hear in the streets are English and Mandarin Chinese.

The Chinese community in Vancouver is very large, and Mandarin Chinese is spoken as a first language in about 30 percent of the homes in Vancouver. There has been a Chinese community in British Columbia for a long time, but it grew a great deal when many people came from Hong Kong in the 1980s. The Chinese community is now so large that many people call the city "Hongcouver."

The Chinese are not the only nonwhite community in Vancouver. In fact, the white population makes up only 51 percent of the city's residents. The largest group after the Chinese are people from India in Southeast Asia, but there are also significant numbers of people from countries such as Vietnam and Korea.

Mini-project City guide

4 **Write a city guide about the city of your choice.**

Choose a city that you know something about and/or are interested in. It could be a city in your own country or somewhere else in the world. Research on the Internet and find information about things like:

- its location
- its geographical features (e.g., is it on a river or near the ocean or mountains?)
- its climate
- its population (ethnic mix)
- the language(s) that people speak

Write a text about the city you have chosen. Find/download photographs that can illustrate the main points of your text.

Crazy collections

1 **Look at the photo and the text. What does this man collect? When did he start? Read the text and check your answers.**

Mister Sandman

When he goes on vacation, Nick D'Errico isn't interested in the sun and watersports. His only interest is … sand! We asked him when his fascination with sand started.

Many years ago. My wife and I were on a vacation in Jamaica, on our honeymoon. One day we were on the beach. The sand was really beautiful and my wife asked me if we could take some of it home. She thought it would be a nice souvenir. I wasn't thinking of starting a new hobby, but I've been collecting sand since that vacation.

How did the hobby start?
Friends started bringing me sand from a lot of exotic countries. When I looked at the sand through a microscope, I saw that there were a lot of different kinds. I was fascinated, and that's how the hobby started. Now it takes up most of my free time.

Have you collected every kind of sand?
Well, I don't know how many kinds of sand there are in the world! But I've collected between 18,000 and 19,000 different kinds. Last year a geology professor in North Carolina asked me if I wanted his collection. Of course, I said yes! His collection weighs 2,722 kilos. It's still in the packages it arrived in. It's taken over my house!

Do you know what the most expensive sand in the world is?
Probably moon sand. Not long ago some moon sand was stolen. It hasn't appeared on the black market yet. But when it does, it will be very, very expensive!

Can you tell me how to start if I want to become a sand collector?
Just go to a beach and stand there. Take your time and look closely. Take sand from different places on the beach. When you see how different all the kinds of sand are, your fascination will start.

How many members does the Sand Society have?
It started with six people. But it's been growing all the time for almost 40 years. Since it started, 240 people have joined from 14 different countries.

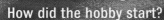

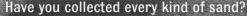

In this unit

You learn
- present perfect continuous
- embedded questions
- words for hobbies and pastimes

and then you can
- talk about collecting something
- talk about hobbies

2 Circle the correct word in each sentence.

1 Nick collects *sand* / *DVDs*.
2 Nick and his wife were on their honeymoon in *Hawaii* / *Jamaica*.
3 Nick's friends brought him sand from different *countries* / *cities*.
4 Nick has collected more than *18,000* / *19,000* kinds of sand.
5 He has a sand collection that *his wife* / *a professor* gave him.
6 The collection is still in packages in *his house* / *North Carolina*.
7 The most expensive sand is probably *moon sand* / *black sand*.
8 The Sand Society has members from *14* / *240* different countries.

Get talking Talking about collecting something

12

3 Listen and act out the dialogue.

A What's your hobby?
B Collecting stamps.
A How long have you been collecting them?
B Since 2002.
A How many do you have?
B About 600.
A Wow! That's a lot.

4 Play a game with a partner. Choose one of the people below. Make dialogues to find out who your partner is thinking of.

A I'm thinking of a girl.
B What's her hobby?
A Collecting records.
B How long has she been collecting them?
A For eight years.
B How many does she have?
A About 300.
B It's Anne Marie.
A That's right.

> **Note:**
> Remember the use of *for* and *since*:
> *for* 4 weeks / 2 months / 3 years
> *since* my last birthday / August / 2004

Alan	Ken	Caroline	Barbara	Karen	Stewart
stamps	baseball cards	coins	seashells	stamps	model planes
3 years	a year	2 years	last vacation	3 years	a long time
about 800	about 130	about 150	about 60	about 200	about 130

Anne Marie	Rick	Jonathan	Nick	Chris	Carl
records	comic books	old books	stamps	stuffed animals	coins
8 years	half a year	2 years	3 years	10 years	2 months
about 300	about 40	about 100	about 200	about 60	about 100

Brenda	Claudia	Lisa	Sue	Simon	Claire
seashells	football pictures	comic books	comic books	records	model planes
last summer	6 months	last year	many years	3 years	2 years
about 120	about 200	about 70	about 450	about 200	about 90

5 Work with a partner. Act out similar dialogues about yourselves.

Language Focus

Vocabulary Hobbies and pastimes

13 **1** Match the activity to the correct photo. Then listen and check.

doing puzzles ☐	going bird-watching ☐	fixing things ☐
taking pictures ☐	keeping a blog ☐	doing pottery ☐
making models ☐	collecting things ☐	playing online games ☐

1
2
3 Blogger

4
5
6

7
8
9

Get talking Talking about hobbies

2 Work with a partner. Ask and answer questions about hobbies.

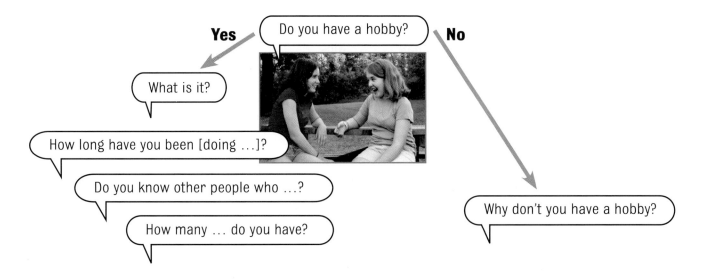

Yes Do you have a hobby? **No**

What is it?

How long have you been [doing ...]?

Do you know other people who ...?

How many ... do you have?

Why don't you have a hobby?

Grammar

Present perfect continuous

1 **Put the words in order to make sentences. Check against the text on page 94.**

collecting / since / sand / vacation / been / that / I've /
almost / 40 years. / been / for / The Sand Society / growing / has /

Use the present perfect continuous to talk about situations that started in the past and are still going on now. You also use it to stress how long an activity has been going on.

This is how you form the **present perfect continuous**:
Person + **have (has)** + **(n't)** + **been** + **ing** form of verb

He**'s been playing** football for two hours.
He **hasn't been studying** for a week.

This is how you form questions:
(Question word) + **have** + **person** + **been** + **ing** form of verb
What **have you been doing**?
How long **have you been collecting** sea shells?

2 **Write sentences to answer the questions.**

(collect / six years)
Why does he have so many CDs?
He's been collecting CDs for
six years.

(eat ice cream / an hour)
Why is she feeling sick?
....
....

(lie in the sun / six hours)
Why is he sunburned?
....
....

(wait for the bus / four o'clock)
Why is she angry?
....
....

(study / this morning)
Why is she tired?
....
....

(ride his bike / all day)
Why is he thirsty?
....
....

3 **Write sentences in the present perfect continuous.**

1 running around / the / yard / been / all morning. / They've ....

2 playing / have / in a band? / you / been / How long ....

3 hours. / to call / for / We've / her / trying / been ....

4 been / San Francisco / years. / They've / living / 12 / in / for ....

Embedded questions

(4) **Which sentence is correct? Check on page 94 if necessary.**

a) I don't know how many kinds of sand there are in the world.
b) I don't know how many kinds of sand are there in the world.

Embedded questions are questions that are hidden in a sentence.
They often begin with *I don't know ......*, *Nobody knows ......*, *I have no idea ......*, etc.

(5) **Read the embedded questions (1–4). Match them to the correct question (a–d).**

1 I don't know when the store opens.
2 Nobody can tell me how much this costs.
3 I'm not sure how many songs I have.
4 Nobody knows when he'll be back.

a) How many songs do you have?
b) When will he be back?
c) How much does this cost?
d) When does the store open?

We'll never find out where the gorilla's hiding.

This is how you form embedded questions:

Question:	Where has he gone?
Embedded question:	I have no idea *where he's gone.*
Question:	How old is it?
Embedded question:	Nobody knows *how old it is.*

(6) **Complete the answers.**

1 "What's her name?" "Sorry, I don't know .....*What her name is.*........."
2 "Where does he live?" "Sorry, I don't know ...."
3 "When did they arrive?" "Sorry, I don't know ...."
4 "Where has he gone?" "Sorry, I don't know ...."
5 "What time is it?" "Sorry, I don't know ...."

(7) **Write one sentence with an embedded question for each pair of sentences.**

1 What would you like to eat? I'm not sure.   *I'm not sure what I'd like to eat.*...............................
2 How old is she? I have no idea.   ....
3 Where did he go? Nobody knows.   ....
4 Is it cold outside? We need to check.   ....
5 Did she call? I don't know.   ....
6 When does the movie start? I'm not sure.   ....

Skills

Listening

14 **1** Listen to the conversation. Paul is asking about Monica's collection. Check (✓) the things Monica collects.

15 **2** Listen to the conversation again. Then circle the correct answer.

1 Monica started her collection *exactly /* (*about*) six years ago.
2 She was on a *road / train* trip with her parents in New England.
3 She took the pens home *as presents for her friends / to start a collection.*
4 Now Monica has *two thousand / five hundred and fifty* pens in her collection.
5 Monica's *parents / friends and their parents* bring pens back for her from their vacations.
6 Pens are easy to bring back because they're *cheap / light.*
7 Her favorite pen is from an expensive hotel in *Paris / San Francisco.*
8 Her favorite pen is made of *metal / plastic.*

Reading

3 Read the texts and answer these questions.

1 When did each of these people start collecting?
2 How many things have they collected so far?
3 When and why did they start their collections?

Marcela T. is 30 years old and works as a photographer in Buenos Aires, Argentina. She has an unusual hobby: she collects tea bags. She started her hobby five years ago when she was on vacation in England with her husband. They were sitting in a tearoom and had ordered some tea. The waiter brought a pot of hot water and a wooden box with a lot of different tea bags. Marcela, who had never really looked at tea bags before, began to study them carefully. She saw how colorful and attractive they were. So she asked friends to bring tea bags back from their vacations, too. So far, Marcela has collected more than 5,000 tea bags from 49 different countries. "Hopefully, my collection will keep on growing," she says.

John M. is 26 years old, and he has an unusual hobby. He collects bathroom faucets. He started collecting them after he turned 20, when he was working as a plumber. He saw bathrooms in many different houses, and thought it was interesting how many different kinds of faucets people had. So one day he started collecting them. Since then he has collected more than 600 faucets. "Unfortunately, when my collection really started growing, there wasn't enough space in my house to keep all of them," says John, "so I rented an old factory to keep them in." John's friends think he is crazy, but of course John doesn't agree with them. He just thinks he has an interesting hobby!

4 **Who is each sentence about, Marcela or John? Circle the correct name.**

1 *Marcela / John* started collecting six years ago.
2 *Marcela / John* gets help from friends.
3 *Marcela / John* started collecting while working.
4 *Marcela / John* started collecting during a vacation.
5 *Marcela / John* doesn't keep the collection in the house.

5 **Circle T (True) or F (False) for the sentences below.**

1 Marcela started collecting tea bags at home. T / F
2 Marcela started collecting tea bags because she liked the colors. T / F
3 Marcela wants her collection to get bigger. T / F
4 John received a bathroom faucet as a present on his birthday. T / F
5 John has 300 faucets. T / F
6 John doesn't think his hobby is crazy. T / F

Speaking

6 **Which collection is more/less interesting, Marcela's or John's? Why?**

7 **Interview three classmates about collecting things.**

Have you ever collected anything?   How long have you had your collection of … ?
What was it?   How long did you collect … ?
When did you collect … ?   How many … did you collect?
                                          Do you still have any … ?

8 **Report to the class.**

I interviewed three classmates. One collected … when she was …
She still has …
One collects … He has collected … since/for …
He has …
One has never collected anything.

Writing

9 **Write a text about an unusual collector.**

- Search the Internet for collectors of unusual things.
- Write a text of about 150 words about a real collector. Write another one about a collector you invent.
- When you have finished, work in small groups. Do not tell one another which of your texts is about an imagined collector and which is about a real one.
- Read all the texts in the group and talk about which of the people you think are real or imagined.

Check your progress   Units 9 and 10

1   **Complete the words.**

1 m _ _ _ solo artist
2 number 1
    s _ _ _ _ _
3 f _ _ _ _ _ solo artist
4 number 1
    a _ _ _ _

☐ **4**

2   **Reorder the letters and write the words.**

1 doing **zusplez** ....
2 making **typetor**
    ....
3 making **seldom**
    ....
4 playing **linnoe**
    games ....
5 **ginxfi** things ....
6 keeping a **glob**
    ....
7 **gnectilloc** things
    ....
8 taking **ciptsrue**
    ....

☐ **8**

3   **Complete the dialogue.**

Max Who's your ¹............ singer?
Zoë I don't know. Maybe Akon.
Max Don't you like Kanye West ²............ ?
Zoë No, not really. I ³............ to like him, didn't I?
Max You were crazy about him! How long have you ⁴............ listening to Akon?
Zoë About a year.
Max How many of his albums ⁵............ you got?
Zoë Only two.

☐ **5**

4   **Complete with *used to* and the words in parentheses.**

1 We .... in Canada. (live)
2 Pablo .... jazz, but he does now. (not / like)
3 What .... to when you were 10? (you / listen)
4 .... long hair? (your brother / have)
5 Do you remember what .... you when you were a baby? (your parents / call).

☐ **5**

5   **Complete the sentences with the words below.**

| to seeing   on paying   at remembering |
| into playing   of going   on starting |
| in joining   of going |

1 Ken's a fan .... to live concerts.
2 I'm really looking forward .... them live.
3 I'm planning .... a collection of CDs.
4 Don always insists .... the check.
5 Are you interested .... our band?
6 I'm bad .... people's birthdays.
7 We're thinking .... for a pizza.
8 My brother's .... loud music!

☐ **8**

6   **Rewrite the sentences using the present perfect continuous and *for/since*.**

1 Vicky started collecting clothes in 2004.
    ....
2 I only started listening to them last week.
    ....
3 He started making records 30 years ago.
    ....
4 I started downloading it this morning.
    ....
5 I started learning Chinese four years ago.
    ....
6 They started playing the game yesterday.
    ....

☐ **12**

7   **Write embedded questions.**

1 What's that fan club called?
    I don't know ....
2 Where can I find out more about this hobby?
    I'm not sure ....
3 What did he die of?
    Nobody knows ....
4 When's the new album coming out?
    Can you ask your brother ....
    ....

☐ **8**

TOTAL ☐ **50**

My progress so far is ...

☺   ☺   ☹
great! ☐   good. ☐   poor. ☐

Unusual collections

1 Read the text and decide if the sentences below are **T** (True) or **F** (False).

An unusual collection

On a family vacation at the age of eight, Jessie Thompson was playing on the beach when she found a strange-looking rock. It was the first of a collection which now includes more than 2,000 items.

In the beginning, Jessie chose to collect rocks because of their shape or color. "I would pick up anything that looked unusual," she says. "Some of my friends were collecting stamps, which I thought was boring. I like collecting rocks because it's something that gets me out of the house. And now that I have learned a little about geology, my collection is even more fascinating. It's really interesting to discover why my rocks are different, where they came from, how they were formed, and that sort of thing. I might even become a geologist one day."

Lately, Jessie has added some crystals and fossils to her collection. She says that her crystals can be found in many places but "are worth more to me than diamonds, and are just as beautiful." Fossils, she says, are a new passion. "I love the idea that I'm holding millions of years of history in my hand." With the help of books and the Internet, Jessie now plans her vacations around where she might find something unusual. "It's not so much left to chance now, but that doesn't mean I won't pick up a rock and put it in my pocket just because it looks cool."

1 Jessie had collected 2,000 rocks by the time she was eight. T/F
2 The first rocks she collected were strange or unusual ones. T/F
3 She used to collect stamps before she started her collection of rocks. T/F
4 She has made a career out of her hobby. T/F
5 Her crystals are worth a lot of money. T/F
6 Jessie's vacations are spent looking for things to add to her collection. T/F

Do you know?

The first steam train was built in 1804 in Wales. It carried 10 tons of iron, 70 people and 5 extra wagons. It traveled 9 miles and the journey took 2 hours.

16 **2** Listen and then answer the questions about collecting toy trains.

1 Where is the National Toy Train Museum?
2 What is *e-Train* magazine?
3 How many members does the Train Collectors Association have?
4 Where do the group's members live?
5 What kinds of trains do people usually collect?
6 Have you ever been on a train?

3 **Over 2 U!** In groups, discuss things you collect or would like to collect.

 **American MORE!** Now you can watch Episode 5 of *School Reporters!*

Museum of Dirt

"Found stuff" is the collection obsession of Glenn Johanson

Glenn Johanson collects "dirt" from all kinds of far-flung places, such as the Great Wall of China, a desert in Saudi Arabia, Aruba, the Amazon River, and many others.

Johanson's dirt specimens are placed in glass jars and labeled, for example, "Dirt from Antarctica" or "Dirt from the Beverly Hillbillies Mansion." Plus he has collected lint, rocks, and other found objects, such as shells from the Great Barrier Reef in Australia and lava from Mt. Fuji in Japan.

Johanson's collection of more than 300 vials of dirt is on display at Jack Morton Worldwide, a marketing company based in Boston, Massachusetts. Johanson is director of operations at the Learning and Digital Media Offices of the company.

Would you ever collect dirt? Try to imagine what kind of dirt might be important to you!

Great Wall of China

Saudi Arabia

Amazon River

Aruba

For MORE! Go to www.cambridge.org/elt/americanmore and take a quiz on this text.

In this unit

You learn
- reported speech
- reported questions
- adjectives for personality

and then you can
- check what people do / explain what you do
- describe people

  1 **Listen and read.**

Interviewer	So Katya. You're a journalist in your free time, aren't you?
Katya	Yes, that's right. I do interviews for *Children's Express*. It's a news magazine run by kids.
Interviewer	Tell me more.
Katya	Well, basically any young person can write a story and send it in. Last year more than 500 kids did something for *Children's Express*.
Interviewer	And what do you do for it?
Katya	Well my favorite thing is doing interviews. For example, a month ago I did an interview with two brave teenagers from Texas who are trying to stop animal testing at a local cosmetics company. They told me they planned a big demonstration outside the laboratories a few weeks ago. They're very patient because they know it will take a long

time, but they are also very determined and they said they would definitely continue to do all they can to stop it.

Interviewer So do you always do political stories?

Katya Oh no. I do all kinds of stories. Only last week I talked to a 14-year-old boy who has to take care of his mother who is a diabetic. He told me that his life was hard, but he said that he could see a light at the end of the tunnel. He was very positive. It was a very inspirational story.

Interviewer So how do you choose the stories you want to do?

Katya I like stories that have a message. I want young people to be more tolerant. I want them to think about how good their lives are. That's why I do the interviews.

2 **Circle the correct word to complete the sentences.**

1 Katya works as a journalist for a news *program / magazine*.
2 *Children's Express* reporters are *adults / kids*.
3 Katya did an interview with *two / three* protest organizers.
4 Katya prefers writing stories about *politics / a lot of different topics*.
5 Last week she talked to a boy who takes care of his *brother / mother*.
6 The boy was feeling *good / bad* about the future.
7 Katya wants her readers to *accept / be more tolerant of* other people.

Get talking Checking what people do / explaining what you do

18

3 **Match the dialogues with the correct pictures. Then listen and repeat.**

1 Boy You're a good artist, aren't you?
  Girl Well, I like to paint when I have the time.

2 Girl You're a volunteer, aren't you?
  Boy That's right. I help at a nursing home on Saturdays.

3 Girl You're in a band, aren't you?
  Boy Yes, I play the drums.

4 Boy You're good at public speaking, aren't you?
  Girl I'm alright. I'm a member of the debate team.

4 **Work with a partner. Use the prompts to make similar dialogues.**

1 a good cook? – help mother in the kitchen
2 baseball fan? – watch games on TV
3 an animal lover? – have three dogs, two cats
4 good at English? – get 98% in last test
5 a long-distance runner – run a marathon last week
6 poet – write poems sometimes

Language Focus

Vocabulary Personality adjectives

1 **Match the sentences with their endings.**

1 Tony doesn't judge other people. He accepts everyone. He's ...   a) considerate
2 Brian's not scared of anything. He's very ...   b) tolerant
3 Adriana loves doing new things. She's ...   c) positive
4 Simon always does the right thing. He's very ...   d) brave
5 Carl thinks about other people. He's ...   e) adventurous
6 Sharon doesn't like being the center of attention. She's ...   f) responsible
7 Susie often shows how she is feeling. She's ...   g) sensitive
8 Poppy always sees the good in everything. She's so ...   h) shy

scared
negative
intolerant
unadventurous
insensitive
outgoing
careless
selfish

2 **Now say the opposites of the adjectives. Choose from the words on the left.**

3 **Read the story. Use adjectives to describe Bob, Lucy, Jessica, Kevin, and Cyril.**

When the plane crashed into the ocean, the survivors were lucky. There was a small island near them and they all swam there. Bob wanted to get rescued immediately. He ran into the forest to get wood to start a fire. Nobody saw him again. After that Cyril didn't want to go anywhere. He just sat on the beach shouting "Somebody save us!" He didn't want to listen to anyone else's plans.
Jessica wanted to explore every part of the island to see what food she could find. She was sure they could find a lot of things to eat. She quickly made friends with the others and created a hunting party. Kevin tried to cheer other people up by saying that everything would be alright. Lucy didn't say anything to anyone. She just waited for a good signal and then called emergency services on her cell phone.

A   I think Bob is impatient because he didn't wait.

B   Yes, and he is careless because he went into the jungle by himself.

Get talking Describing people

4 **Put the dialogue in order. Then listen and repeat.**

..... **A** Why do you say that?
..... **A** Do you have a sister?
..... **A** What's she like?
..... **B** She waits for hours while I get ready to go out, and she never complains.
..... **B** Yes I do. Her name's Helen.
..... **B** She's a little shy, but very tolerant.

Grammar

Reported speech

1 **Complete the table. Use the dialogue on page 104.**

Direct speech	Reported speech
"My life is hard."	He told me that [1]....... life [2]...... hard
"We planned a big demonstration ."	They told me [3]....... .... a big demonstration.
"We will do all we can to stop it."	They said [4]....... .... do all they can to stop it.
"I can see a light at the end of the tunnel."	He said that [5]....... .... see a light at the end of the tunnel.

Rules

When we want to report what someone has said, we commonly use the verbs *say* and *tell*.
Notice the different ways we use them.
He said (that)...
He told me (that)... (With *tell* we use an object)

We also often change the tense used in the original sentence.

simple present → simple past	*will → would*
present continuous → past continuous	*can → could*
past/present perfect → past perfect	*is/are going to → was/were going to*

Remember to change the pronouns if necessary.

2 **Here are some of the things one of the teenagers from Texas told Katya. Change the reported speech back into the words he said.**

1 He said that he was really angry. ...*I'm really angry.*...

2 He told me he was going to write a letter to the president. ....

3 He said he would fight until the laboratory was closed. ....

4 He told me that they loved animals. ....

5 He said that they had a lot of support from the local people. ....

6 He told me they were planning another demonstration. ....

7 He told me that he had spent a lot of time on this case. ....

8 He said that they hadn't heard anything from the company yet. ....

3 **Here are some more things that Katya told the interviewer. Report them using the verb in parentheses.**

1 I work for a news magazine. (say)
She said that she worked for a news magazine.

2 I'm just finishing my latest story. (tell)
....

3 I've met a lot of famous people. (say)
....

4 I interviewed George Clooney last year. (tell)
....

5 I'm going to interview Madonna soon. (say)
....

6 I'll send you a copy of my interview. (tell)
....

7 I can show you where I work. (say)
....

8 I was very happy with my last story. (tell)
....

Reported questions

4 **Look at the examples of reported questions.**

1 I asked them if that would be dangerous   2 I asked them why they were here

Put the words in order to make the original questions.

a) it / dangerous / be / will / ?   b) are / ? / why / here / you

Rules

When we report questions, we use the verb "ask someone (if/whether)" or "wonder" or "want to know." If the question has a question word such as "when/how/why/who/what/where" in it, we use the same question word in the reported question.

If the question is a Yes/No question (= it *doesn't* have a question word) we use the word "if" in the reported question.

We *don't* use auxiliaries such as "do/does" in reported questions—the word order is like a statement, not a question. (e.g. He asked me what I wanted; **not** He asked me ~~what did I want~~) The tense of the verb in the question usually changes.

5 **Write the original questions.**

1 He asked me what my name was. ..*What's your name?*...
2 He asked me if I was Spanish. ....
3 He asked why I wanted to study English. ....
4 He asked me if I had studied English at school. ....
5 He asked me if I had visited the U.S. before. ....
6 He asked me how long I was going to stay in the U.S. ....

6 **Put the words in the correct order.**

1 asked / My father / if / me / I / the answer / knew ..*My father asked me if I knew the answer.*...
2 hungry / She / if / was / I / asked / me ....
3 asked / her / if / Steve / wanted / ice cream / she ....
4 We / where / asked / her / she / bought / her shoes / had ....
5 I / what / her telephone number / asked / was / her ....
6 movie / him / if / She / before / asked / seen / had / the / he ....
7 I / where / him / was / going / he / asked ....
8 her / if / He / asked / some / she / help / homework / with / her / wanted ....

7 **Complete the reported questions.**

1 "How old are you?"   She asked me ...*how old*... I was.
2 "Where do you live?"   They asked me .... I lived.
3 "Where did you buy them?"   I asked her .... she had bought them.
4 "Do you want to come with us?"   We asked him .... to come with us.
5 "Are you American?"   They asked me ....
6 "Have you ever been to Greece?"   He asked me ....
7 "When did you graduate?"   He asked her ....
8 "Who bought you the flowers?"   He asked me ....

Skills

Reading

1 Read Joanne's poem and choose the best title for it from the titles below.

Fitting in   No more tears   Me   Odd one out

When I was in junior high school, I really wanted to fit in. But I never did. There were these two girls who made my life miserable. They told stories about me to the other kids, their moms, and even the teachers. Everybody hated me and I cried myself to sleep almost every night. Things got better when I moved to another school when I was 15. I made wonderful friends there and now I'm happy. I wrote a poem about it. In fact, I write a lot of poetry. It helps me with any problems I have.

I had always been the odd one out
I had never belonged to a crowd
and I had never sat with the popular girls
during school lunches,
watching the others
looking at us.

I had always wanted the popular kids
to ask me to their parties,
to whisper with me during lunch break,
to share yesterday's stories
and tomorrow's plans.

It never happened.

Now after years of crying,
of being the odd one out,
I'm a different girl
because I'm the one
who speaks out.

I'm no longer the girl they can bully,
I'm no longer the odd one out,
I was lucky because I have met—me.

2 Read the poem again and decide if the sentences are T (True) or F (False).

1 The poet was bullied by three girls at school.   T / F
2 Other students spread lies about the poet.   T / F
3 The poet felt happier at her new school.   T / F
4 The poet writes because it helps her feel better.   T / F
5 She went to a lot of parties.   T / F
6 She felt like she didn't have anyone to share things with.   T / F
7 She became happier when the other girls accepted her.   T / F
8 The poet believes it's important to know yourself.   T / F

Listening and speaking

3 Listen to Samir, Jonathan, and Helen talking about their lives. Which of these things do they *not* mention?

☐ school ☐ football ☐ TV ☐ problems
☐ shopping ☐ fighting ☐ music ☐ friends

4 Listen again and check (✓) the correct answers.

1 Jonathan thinks
   ☐ boys are smarter than girls.
   ☐ boys and girls watch the same things on TV.
   ☐ the differences between boys and girls aren't really very big.

2 Helen thinks
   ☐ girls are good at solving problems.
   ☐ girls and boys aren't very different.
   ☐ girls talk more than boys.

3 Helen thinks
   ☐ teenagers should appreciate how good their lives are.

☐ most teenagers have a lot of problems.
☐ wars are irresponsible.

4 Samir
   ☐ gets into a lot of fights.
   ☐ listens to music to relax.
   ☐ never gets angry.

5 Jonathan
   ☐ thinks life is really hard for teenagers.
   ☐ thinks friends are really important.
   ☐ feels depressed sometimes.

5 Here are some opinions expressed in the listening activity. How much do you agree with them? Give each a score from 0 (I disagree 100%) to 5 (I agree 100%).

1 Girls get better grades than boys. ☐
2 Girls are better at solving problems. ☐
3 Girls fight more often than boys. ☐
4 Girls make things more complicated than boys. ☐
5 Music is very important to teenagers. ☐
6 It's always good to share problems with an older person. ☐

6 Work in small groups and compare your answers.

Sounds right Reporting direct speech

22

7 Work in pairs. Listen and repeat. Then practice reporting what Samir, Jonathan, and Helen said.

Jonathan said [pause], "I don't think there are many differences," [pause] and he said [pause], "Well, there are some things..."

(Notice how there is a short pause before and after the quotes. Also the voice is higher on the quotes.)

Reading and writing

8 Read the letters to the "Ask Paula" advice column and match each one to a picture.

❶

Dear Paula,
My younger sister wants to hang out with my friends, but they aren't interested in her. She keeps giving them little presents, and she hangs around in front of their houses and waits for them in the mornings. I know that they laugh at her. I know that they want her to leave them alone. Should I tell her that everyone is laughing at her? Or should I just wait it out?
Yours, Katie

❷

Dear Paula,
There is a teacher at my school who is making my life difficult. She is always picking on me. She tells me off for talking when I'm not. She gives me terrible grades on all my homework. She even sent me to see the principal the other day. I don't know why she is doing this. What can I do? I'm starting to hate going to school.
Yours, Larry

9 Read the replies from Paula. Which letter do you think each one talks about, Katie's or Larry's? Write K or L.

1 You need to find out why she is treating you this way. ☐
2 Talk to your parents. Maybe they can talk to her. ☐
3 If you are a good friend, you have to tell her. ☐
4 Be sensitive. Your sister obviously thinks she's friends with your friends. ☐
5 Remember, one day you might need her help. ☐
6 Are you sure your behavior is always perfect? ☐

10 Write a reply to one of the letters. Use the replies in Exercise 9 to help you.

Understanding poetry

Key words

concrete poetry	shape poem	poetic device
rhyme	alliteration	rhythm
pattern	(un)stressed syllable	

1 **Read about poetry.**

Poetry is art. Writing a poem is like painting a picture that uses words instead of colors. Just like there are different styles and kinds of paintings, poems are different, too. There are some poems, for example, where the shape of how words are arranged somehow also expresses the content. They are called concrete or shape poems. Here is an example:

A
dark
green giant
is standing, silent
as a deserted forest,
in the corner of my room.
A hundred
brightly colored
shiny balls like sparkling
fruit hang from spiky branches.
And tinsel, like a great golden snake,
wraps and curls itself around its body.
But
best
of all
are the presents
piled around its
burnished base.

Other kinds of poems use special techniques known as "poetic devices" to create certain effects in the reader's mind. The following poetic devices are frequently used.

a) Rhyme focuses on the sounds in the end parts of the words (fine, mine, sign).

b) Alliteration is repeating sounds in the first part of the words, such as when the initial consonants of words are repeated (seven swans swimming swiftly).

c) Rhythm focuses on the way stressed and unstressed syllables follow one another, very much like the beat (rhythm) in a song.

2 **Read the following poems. First of all, make sure you understand them. Look up any words you don't understand in a dictionary. Then read the poems aloud to a partner and discuss the questions.**

- Which of the two poems uses rhyme and alliteration as poetic devices?
- Which of the two poems do you like better? Why?

Poem 1:

A fly and a flea flew up in a flue.
Said the fly to the flea, "What shall we do?"
"Let's fly," said the flea.
"Let's flee," said the fly.
So they fluttered and flew up a flaw in the flue.

Poem 2:

Night time
by Lee Bennet Hopkins

How do dreams know
when to creep
into my head
when I fall off
to sleep?

3 **Bringing rhyme and rhythm together: limericks.**

The word *limerick* comes from a town in Ireland. A *limerick* is a short poem that follows a strict poetic form. A *limerick* would not be a *limerick* if it didn't have humor in it and didn't follow clear rules for rhythm and rhyme.

Read the limerick. Then answer the following questions.

(1) A clumsy young fellow named Tim
(2) was never informed how to swim.
(3) He fell off a dock
(4) and sank like a rock.
(5) And that was the end of him.

How many lines does a limerick have?
Which lines in the limerick rhyme with one another?
Match the following patterns of rhythm to the lines of the poem above.

(a)   da DEE da da DEE
(b)   da DEE da da DEE da da DEE or
            da DEE da da DEE da DEE

Mini-project Analyzing a poem

4 **Find a poem in English that you like. Look up all the words you don't understand. Analyze it and look for all the poetic devices used in the poem. Read your poem aloud to the class and give a short report on your analysis.**

5 **Alternatively, use the poem here.**

Don't think rivers,
Don't think fountains,
Don't think mountain streams, or creeks.
Don't think pools or ponds or oceans.
Don't think lakes and don't think leaks.
Don't think wells or wet or water.
Don't think showers.
Don't think springs.
Don't think moist or damp or rainy.
Don't think hurricanes or things
That drizzle, dribble, drip, drop, flood, or flow,
When there's no bathroom—and you gotta go.

© Judith Viorst

1 Listen and read.

Juanita Carlos has a small coffee farm in the hills of Honduras. She gets up at daybreak, has breakfast, and then starts working in the fields. She works very hard, and goes to bed late, but she has little money—just enough to buy food and clothes for herself and her two children. She also takes care of her elderly mother. She doesn't have a car, and she doesn't have a TV. She would buy those things if she got more money for her coffee. Juanita listens to the radio every morning. She wants to hear what they say about the price of coffee in faraway New York City. The news she hears is usually bad. Coffee prices are low, and Juanita is very worried.

"If I had known that coffee prices would go down so much, I would have sold the farm a long time ago," Juanita says. Where Juanita lives, all the small farmers and their families are as poor as she is.

Ramon Machado's farm is only three hours away from Juanita's. Ramon is

not as worried as Juanita, and he doesn't listen to the radio every morning to find out about coffee prices.

That's because Ramon and 20 other farmers are part of a "Fair Trade" project. They get a fixed price for their coffee. But the project is not only about paying farmers a fair price for their products. Members of the Fair Trade project do not use pesticides. On their small farms there are a lot of trees that give shade to the coffee plants. Among them there are banana trees and avocado trees. This is good for the environment.

Ramon joined the project a year ago. Now he is happy because he doesn't have to worry about feeding his children or buying them clothes or books for school. If other farmers got a fixed price for their coffee, too, their situation would be much better.

In this unit

You learn
- *If*-clauses (review)
- words for workplaces

and then you can
- talk about what you would have done
- talk about places

2 Complete the sentences about Juanita and Ramon.

1 Juanita has a small .... in ....
2 She works very ...., but ....
3 She doesn't have a car or a ....
4 Every morning she listens to .... because she ....
5 Ramon is not as worried about .... as .... is.
6 Ramon doesn't listen ....
7 Ramon gets a fixed ....
8 Ramon is part of a ....

Get talking Talking about what you would have done

24 **3** Read the dialogue. Write the correct name—Alan, Paula, Max, or Grace—under the person. Then listen and repeat.

1 ....   2 ....   3 ....   4 ....

Don So I was walking down the street when this huge dog ran in front of me. I didn't know what to do.
Alan I would've run away.
Paula I would've thrown a stick for it.
Max I would've shouted at it.
Grace I would've walked past it.

4 Work in groups of three. Take turns to describe the situation and say what you would have done. Use the prompts to help you.

1 The soup came and it was cold.
   send it back / not eat it

   A I would've sent it back.

   B I wouldn't have eaten it.

2 I lent Joe my CD and he lost it.
   ask for a new one / tell him not to worry about it

3 I had a really important test.
   study hard / not study and hope for the best

4 I knocked on his door, but he didn't answer.
   go home / call his cell phone

Language Focus

Vocabulary Workplaces

1 Match these people to the places where they work. Write the correct number in the box.

- ☐ a gym
- ☐ a hotel
- ☐ a mine
- ☐ a factory
- ☐ an office
- ☐ a warehouse
- ☐ a laboratory
- ☐ a prison
- ☐ a courtroom
- ☐ a farm

1 farmer

2 miner

3 factory worker

4 scientist

5 judge

6 office worker

7 prison guard

8 warehouse worker

9 porter

10 fitness instructor

2 Choose one of the workers in Exercise 1. Mime an action that person might do for the other students to guess.

> You're milking a cow.
> You're on a farm.

Get talking Talking about places

3 Read the dialogues and complete them using the words on the left.

where
prison
criminals
factory

A What does your dad do?
B He's a guard. He works in a ¹............
A What's that?
B It's a place where ²............ go.

A What does your mom do?
B She works in a ³...............
A What's that?
B It's a place ⁴.............. people make things.

4 Listen and check. Then practice the dialogues with a partner. [25]

5 Use the prompts to make similar dialogues.

1 miner / mine / dig things out of the ground
2 warehouse worker / warehouse / keep things before they go to the stores
3 scientist / laboratory / do experiments
4 fitness instructor / gym / do exercise

Grammar

If-clauses (review)

First conditional

Use the first conditional to talk about things that are in the future.
If-clause: If + subject + simple present, **Main clause:** subject + **will/won't** + infinitive

1 **Match the sentence halves.**

1 If more farmers stop using pesticides,
2 If more farmers join the Fair Trade projects,
3 If you listen to the news,

a) you'll find out more about the situation.
b) it would be good for the environment.
c) they won't have to worry about coffee prices.

Note: the If-clause and main clause often switch position.
The main clause can come before the If-clause.

2 **Complete each sentence with the correct form of the verb in parentheses.**

1 If you have time, I .... you my new computer. (show)
2 They'll get angry if they .... the news. (hear)
3 Mom .... you more allowance if you only buy candy. (not give)
4 Our team .... the game if they continue playing so well. (win)
5 If it is really his birthday on Monday, I .... him a nice present. (buy)
6 If he doesn't answer my emails, I .... to him again. (not write)

Second conditional

We use the second conditional to talk about situations that we don't expect to happen or that are unreal.
If-clause: If + subject + simple past, **Main clause:** subject + **would ('d)/wouldn't** + infinitive
If Juanita got more money for her coffee, she would (she'd) buy a car.

3 **Which statement is correct?**

a) Juanita has a car because she is getting a better price for her coffee.
b) Juanita doesn't have the money to buy a car.

4 **Read aloud the sentences. Use the correct forms.**

1 If I *would have / had* more time, I *would go / went* to the movies with you.
2 If all farmers *would hear / heard* about Fair Trade projects, it *would be / was* good.
3 *We'd help / We helped* you with your homework if we *knew / would know* the answers.
4 If Peter *would play / played* tennis, he *was / would be* fitter.
5 She *were / would be* very angry if she *heard / would hear* what you said.
6 If I *would be / were* you, *I'd work / I work* harder.

5 Complete each sentence with the correct form of the verb in parentheses.

1 What would you say if I .... you this camera as a present? (give)
2 I .... not .... that if I were you. (not do)
3 The computer .... a lot more expensive if you wanted a bigger screen. (be)
4 If I had her phone number, I'......................... it to you. (give)
5 If I .... $1,000, I'd buy a new mountain bike. (have)
6 They'd buy a bigger house if they .... the money. (have)

6 Read the sentences and say if they are first or second conditionals.

1 I'll buy it if I have enough money. ....   4 If you ate that, you'd die. ....
2 I'd buy it if I had enough money. ....   5 If it's a new dress, I'll be really happy. ....
3 If you eat any more, you'll feel sick. ....   6 If it was green, it'd be perfect. ....

Second conditional questions

To ask a question using the second conditional you simply reverse the word order.
You would buy Fair Trade products if a local store sold them.

Would you buy Fair Trade products if a local store sold them?

---

7 Match the questions and answers.

1 What would you buy if I gave you $500?   a) Of course I would.
2 Would you help me if I asked you?   b) She would if you invited her.
3 Where would you like to live?   c) I'd bring it back tomorrow if you lent it to me.
4 Would Sarah come to the party?   d) Anywhere near the ocean.
5 How long would you need my bike?   e) A new cell phone.
6 Which movie star would you like to meet?   f) Penélope Cruz. She does a lot to help others.

8 Put the words in order to make questions.

1 animal / what / like / you / be / would / to *What animal would you like to be?*
2 like / you / to / would / go / vacation / where / for / your ....
3 like / what / you / superpower / to / would / have ....
4 found / on / diamond / you / do / if / you / a / floor / would / ring / what / the ....
5 like / person / famous / what / would / you / to / meet ....
6 like / question / person / would / one / you / what / to / this / ask ....

9 Work with a partner. Ask the questions from Exercise 8. Take turns to answer each one.

A What animal would you like to be?   **B** I'd like to be a dolphin.

Skills

Listening

 1 Look at the pictures. Number them in the correct order to tell a story. Then listen and check.

Reading

 2 Read Jessica's journal entry about an unfair situation at school.

I'll never forget what happened to me today in history class. We had a new teacher, Mr. Twaine. He's very young, and it was our first class with him. Nick wanted to make life difficult for him. Mr. Twaine turned his back to us to write something on the board, and Nick started to make little balls of paper, which he started to throw at the teacher! When the teacher turned around to check who it was, Nick stopped, of course. This went on for some time, and the whole class started to laugh. I didn't think it was funny at all.

Anyway, Mr. Twaine kept on talking, and he was still very friendly. When he turned his back to the class again, suddenly it happened. One of Nick's paper balls landed on my head. I was furious. I picked it up and threw it back at Nick. Suddenly Mr. Twaine turned around and saw me throwing the paper ball!

He looked at me for a long time, and then he said, "Don't you think throwing paper balls is a little childish? Stop it now and pick up all the balls from the floor." He was pretty angry. What should I have done? If I said it wasn't me, would the teacher believe me? After all, he had seen me throw the paper. If I said it was Nick, Nick would be angry. I wouldn't like that. So I got up from my seat and picked up all the paper balls from the floor. Nick was sitting there smiling. I thought that was really unfair!

3 Circle T (True) or F (False) for the sentences below.

1 The story happened two years ago in Jessica's history class. T / F
2 It was Mr. Twaine's first time teaching Jessica's class. T / F
3 Nobody found it funny when Nick threw little balls of paper. T / F
4 Jessica was furious because Nick hit her friend Sandra on her head. T / F
5 Mr. Twaine said that throwing paper balls was childish. T / F

Speaking

4 Match the words to make phrases.
Check your answers with a partner.

1	have	a)	the hospital
2	go to	b)	basketball
3	study	c)	food
4	fail	d)	an accident
5	grow	e)	prison
6	play	f)	hard
7	steal	g)	a test
8	go to	h)	coffee

5 Read the situations. Do you think they are fair or unfair? Give your reasons.

a) A race car driver is in a bad accident. He goes to the hospital, where two nurses help him. The race car driver earns $15 million a year. The nurses each earn $18,000 a year.

b) A girl studies hard for a test and gets a D. Another girl doesn't study for the test at all, but gets an A (without cheating).

c) A coffee farmer in Latin America grows coffee and sells it to a big coffee company for 25 cents per kilogram. The company then sells the coffee in the U.S. for $3.10 a kilogram.

d) A school has a basketball team for girls only. Boys can play on the basketball court in the school, but they can't be on the school team.

e) In a certain country, men and women always get the same pay if they do the same job. Men can stop working when they turn 63. Women can stop working when they turn 60.

f) A man with no job steals some food from a store and he goes to prison for six months. A rock star is caught when he steals a pair of pants from a store. He pays a fine of $10,000.

It's not fair if…

I don't think it's fair when …

That's completely unfair!

I don't think it's unfair at all.

Writing for your Portfolio

6 Think about something fair or unfair that happened to you or that you heard about. Write a journal entry about it.

Check your progress Units 11 and 12

1 Complete the words to make adjectives.

1 consider_ _ _
2 _ _toler_ _ _
3 _ _adventur_ _ _
4 _ _sensit_ _ _
5 responsib_ _

☐ 5

2 Complete the names of the workplaces.

1 Where food is grown and animals are kept.
f_ _ _
2 Where a judge works. c_ _ _ _ r_ _ _
3 Underground where we find coal. m_ _ _
4 Where a lot of things are stored.
w_ _ _ _ _ _ _ _
5 Where scientists do experiments.
l_ _ _ _ _ _ _ _ _

☐ 5

3 Say what you would do if the following happened to you.

1 A letter came to your house by mistake.

....

....

2 Your English teacher gave you a terrible grade on your homework.

....

....

3 Someone said you had stolen some money, but you hadn't.

....

....

4 Somebody helped you with a problem.

....

....

☐ 8

4 Rewrite in reported speech.

1 I'm going out.
She said ....

2 I don't understand.
He said ....

3 I was looking for you.
He told me ....

4 I had an accident.
She told me ....

5 I have seen this somewhere before.
He said ....

☐ 10

5 Write the reported questions.

1 Where did you go?
He ....

2 Do you want some ice cream?
She ....

3 Do you think it will be expensive?
He ....

4 How often do you watch the news on TV?
She ....

☐ 8

6 Choose the correct answers.

1 If people *take / took* action now, we will stop the damage.
2 If we *score / scored* one more goal, we would win.
3 If George *will do / does* that again, I'll scream!
4 It *didn't / wouldn't* happen again if you were careful.
5 I *don't / won't* help you if you are rude.
6 If I *had / have* money, I would go to China.

☐ 6

7 Rewrite in the second conditional.

1 I'm not rich, so I can't buy you a car.
If ....

2 I'm not interested, so I won't buy the DVD.
If ....

3 He doesn't have any money so he can't go on vacation.
If ....

4 He wants to join the army, but he's not old enough.
If ....

☐ 8

TOTAL ☐ 50

My progress so far is ...

☺ 😐 ☹

great! ☐   good. ☐   poor. ☐

Ethical buying!

1 Read the article about buying ethically. Then work with a partner and discuss the questions below.

Buying ethically

You are out shopping with friends, and you find a great new shirt. It's just what you're looking for and it's cheap. But what would you do if you found out that a six-year-old child had made that shirt? Would you put it back or buy it anyway?

Buying ethically means that the things we pay for are not made by people who were paid almost nothing. It means not buying things that were made by children who should be in school. Buying ethically also means that the environment is not damaged in order to make the goods.

Despite this, in many countries around the world, young children spend long days working for terrible pay, sometimes far away from their families. There have been many stories of children—sometimes as young as six—being beaten for not working hard enough. There are also thousands of cases where the environment has been badly damaged by people who only care about money.

How can you help? Next time you are shopping, ask where things were made. There are several organizations that only buy and sell things that have been made using ethical standards. And if you don't think it's worth the effort, ask yourself if you would look good in a shirt that was made by an unhappy, terrified child, or wearing a pair of shoes that were made using chemicals that destroyed that child's village.

1 What does buying ethically mean?
2 What happens when we don't buy ethically?
3 What happens to children who don't work hard?
4 What can we do to help the situation?
5 Why does the writer mention the shirt and shoes at the end?

Do **you** know?

Cotton is the world's dirtiest agricultural product. Cotton farms use more insecticides than any other crop in the world. The toxic chemicals sprayed on cotton crops pollute the land, air, food, and drinking water and can cause health problems. Cotton is also the world's thirstiest crop.

27

2 The information below came from a survey. Guess the percentages and write (e.g. 70%) next to each item. Then listen and check your answers.

People who ...	Percentage
don't care how their clothes are produced.	....
would pay more for ethically-made clothes.	....
want to see an end to child labor.	....
care about damage to the environment.	....
ask about where clothes are made.	....
would like us to use fewer chemicals when making clothes.	....
care more about price than anything else.	....

3 **Over 2 U!** In groups, write questions for an ethical shopping survey. As a class, choose the best questions. Then take the survey in class and with other classes.

American MORE! Now you can watch Episode 6 of *School Reporters!*

Fair? Well ...

(They are in a classroom, working. The bell rings for the end of the class)

Teacher OK, so that's it for today, everyone. But, of course, before you go, here's your homework for tonight ...

James Oh, please! That's not fair!

Teacher Really? How come?

Maggie You've given us homework every day already this week.

Teacher That's right. I have. And?

James And there's the game tonight, sir. You know, the game against East High.

Teacher It's only a game, James. And anyway, you have time before it starts, don't you?

James Yeah, but I wanted to hang out with my friends beforehand.

Teacher So my homework's going to interrupt your evening's entertainment. I am sorry, James. Yes, Maggie. What is it?

Maggie Please don't give us homework tonight.

Teacher Why, Maggie? What are you doing that's so important? Don't tell me you want to watch the game, too!

Maggie No way. But I already have tons of history homework for Mr. Newson for tomorrow.

Teacher So Mr. Newson's allowed to give you homework but I'm not. That's not exactly fair either, is it? When did Mr. Newson give you this homework, anyway?

Maggie On Monday.

Teacher So you've had two days to do your homework and chosen to leave it all until the last minute. That's not exactly my fault, is it?

Maggie Oh, pleeeeease.

Teacher OK. Let's see. If I don't give you homework, you don't study enough. If you don't study enough, you don't pass the exams. If you don't pass the exams, your parents get angry and complain to the principal. And I get the principal complaining to me. And I lose my job. How fair is that?

James That's a little dramatic, I think.

Teacher Well, James, that's because I went to drama school.

Maggie So, did you want to be an actor?

Teacher Yes, I did, but we're not going to talk about that now because I'm going to give you your homework. OK?

James But that's not ...

Teacher ... and if anyone says "That's not fair," they'll get double homework.

James That's double unfair!

Teacher Careful James! Now, let me think. OK, for homework, I want a 500-word essay with the title "Why isn't life fair?"

Maggie *(ironically)* Oh, I get it.

Teacher That's right, Maggie. OK, give it to me in Friday's class. That's two days you've got. Bye everyone. Enjoy the game, James!

For MORE! Go to www.cambridge.org/elt/americanmore and take a quiz on this text.

Wordlist

Unit 1

beliefs /bə'liːfs/
boxes /'baːksɪz/
colony /'kɑːləni/
corn /kɔːrn/
fight /faɪt/
gloves /glʌvz/
goggles /'gɑːgəlz/
harbor /'hɑːrbər/
harvest /'hɑːrvɪst/
helmet /'helmət/
incredible /ɪn'kredəbəl/
merchants /'mɜːrtʃənts/
native /'neɪt̬ɪv/
pads /pædz/
port /pɔːrt/
shorts /ʃɔːrts/
sneakers /'sniːkərz/
socks /sɑːks/
steep hill /ˌstiːp 'hɪl/
successful /sək'sesfəl/
to be lucky /ˌbiː 'lʌki/
to belong /bɪ'lɑːŋ/
to chase /tʃeɪs/
to end up /end 'ʌp/
to grow corn /ˌgroʊ 'kɔːrn/
to pay taxes /ˌpeɪ 'tæksɪz/
to roll /roʊl/
to take part /ˌteɪk 'pɑːrt/
turkey /'tɜːrki/
vest /vest/

Unit 2

bottom /'bɑːt̬əm/
deepest /'diːpɪst/
disgusting /dɪs'gʌstɪŋ/
flight /flaɪt/
grade /greɪd/
height /haɪt/
millions /'mɪljənz/
plaque /plæk/
quiet /'kwaɪət/
rocket /'rɑːkɪt/
seat /siːt/
space shuttle /'speɪs ˌʃʌt̬əl/
sunrise /'sʌnraɪz/
sunset /'sʌnset/

to break up /breɪk 'ʌp/
to carry /'kæri/
to get into /ˌget 'ɪntuː/
to land /lænd/
to race /reɪs/
to reenter /riː'entər/
to risk /rɪsk/
to run out of something
 /ˌrʌn 'aʊt əv .../
to set out /set 'aʊt/
to soak /soʊk/
to step /step/
to strike /straɪk/
top /tɑːp/
vehicles /'viːəkəlz/
weird /wɪrd/

Unit 3

asteroid /'æstərɔɪd/
brand new /ˌbrænd 'nuː/
burning process /'bɜːrnɪŋ
 ˌprɑːses/
challenge /'tʃæləndʒ/
change /tʃeɪndʒ/
credit card /'kredɪt ˌkɑːrd/
debit card /'debɪt ˌkɑːrd/
engine /'endʒɪn/
exhausted /ɪg'zɑːstɪd/
fear /fɪr/
fuel /'fjuːəl/
high-pressure gas /ˌhaɪ
 ˌpreʃər 'gæs/
hose /hoʊz/
launch /lɑːntʃ/
leather /'leðər/
lifestyle /'laɪfstaɪl/
mass /mæs/
secondhand section
 /ˌsekənd'hænd
 ˌsekʃən/
temperature
 /'tempərətʃər/
tiring /'taɪrɪŋ/
to cut up /kʌt 'ʌp/
to exchange /ɪks'tʃeɪndʒ/
to load /loʊd/
to solve a problem
 /ˌsɑːlv ə 'prɑːbləm/
to suppose /sə'poʊz/

to waste /weɪst/
to weigh /weɪ/
wages /'weɪdʒɪz/

Unit 4

ambitious /æm'bɪʃəs/
arrogant /'ærəgənt/
creative /kriː'eɪt̬ɪv/
customers /'kʌstəmərz/
dishwasher /'dɪʃwɑːʃər/
easygoing /ˌiːzi 'goʊɪŋ/
efficient /ɪ'fɪʃənt/
friendly /'frendli/
hardworking
 /ˌhɑːrd'wɜːrkɪŋ/
helpful /'helpfəl/
honest /'ɑːnɪst/
imaginative
 /ɪ'mædʒɪnət̬ɪv/
independent
 /ˌɪndə'pendənt/
kind /kaɪnd/
ladder /'lædər/
morning /'mɔːrnɪŋ/
patient /'peɪʃənt/
peacekeeping force
 /'piːskiːpɪŋ ˌfɔːrs/
polite /pə'laɪt/
responsible
 /rɪ'spɑːnsəbəl/
soldier /'soʊldʒər/
the sight of /ðə 'saɪt əv/
to get ready /ˌget 'redi/
to involve /ɪn'vɑːlv/
to lose /luːz/
to make jokes /ˌmeɪk
 'dʒoʊks/
window washer /'wɪndoʊ
 ˌwɑːʃər/

Unit 5

breeding grounds
 /'briːdɪŋ ˌgraʊndz/
bright /braɪt/
confusing /kən'fjuːzɪŋ/
creatures /'kriːtʃərz/
currents /'kʌrənts/
daylight /'deɪlaɪt/

disappointed
 /ˌdɪsə'pɔɪnt̬ɪd/
dream /driːm/
ending /'endɪŋ/
eyesight /'aɪsaɪt/
parachute /'perəʃuːt/
plankton /'plæŋktən/
predators /'predət̬ərz/
series /'sɪriːz/
steam /stiːm/
thrilling /'θrɪlɪŋ/
to burn /bɜːrn/
to care about something
 /'ker əˌbaʊt .../
to cram into something
 /ˌkræm 'ɪntuː .../
to fall asleep /ˌfɔːl ə'sliːp/
to feed /fiːd/
to give birth /ˌgɪv 'bɜːrθ/
to hang out /hæŋ 'aʊt/
to hurtle /'hɜːrt̬əl/
to insist /ɪn'sɪst/
to jolt /dʒoʊlt/
to knock over something
 /ˌnɑːk 'oʊvər .../
to lay eggs /ˌleɪ 'egz/
to migrate /'maɪgreɪt/
to pick /pɪk/
to put something down
 /pʊt ... 'daʊn/
to recommend
 /ˌrekə'mend/
to run into someone
 /ˌrʌn 'ɪntuː .../
to stand up /stænd 'ʌp/
to take after someone
 /teɪk 'æftər .../
to take up something
 /teɪk 'ʌp .../
to turn up the volume
 /ˌtɜːrn ʌp ðə 'vɑːljuːm/
view /vjuː/
walk out /wɑːk 'aʊt/
waterfalls /'wɑːt̬ərfɔːlz/

Unit 6

bike race /'baɪk ˌreɪs/
book fair /'bʊk ˌfer/
car show /'kɑːr ʃoʊ/

fashion show /'fæʃən ˌʃoʊ/

fireworks /'faɪərwɜːrks/

front page /ˌfrʌnt 'peɪʤ/

movie premiere /'muːvi prɪˌmɪr/

put up the tent /ˌpʊʈ ʌp ðə 'tent/

rock festival /'rɑːk ˌfestɪvəl/

school fair /ˌskuːl 'fer/

strawberries /'strɑːˌberiz/

tennis tournament /'tenɪs ˌtɜːrnəmənt/

to camp /kæmp/

to pick up /pɪk 'ʌp/

to stay overnight /ˌsteɪ oʊvər'naɪt/

Unit 7

artificial /ɑːrʈɪ'fɪʃəl/

baked /beɪkt/

boiled /bɔɪld/

breakdancing /'breɪkˌdænsɪŋ/

broiled /brɔɪld/

decline /dɪ'klaɪn/

diabetes /ˌdaɪə'biːʈiːz/

fattening /'fæʈənɪŋ/

filling /'fɪlɪŋ/

fried /fraɪd/

graffiti /grə'fiːʈi/

grilled /grɪld/

harmful /'hɑːrmfəl/

health /helθ/

healthy /'helθi/

mild /maɪld/

moody /'muːdi/

movement /'muːvmənt/

nutritious /nuː'trɪʃəs/

obese /oʊ'biːs/

popularity /pɑːpjə'lærəʈi/

raw /rɑː/

rich /rɪʧ/

roasted /roʊst/

salsa /'sɑːlsə/

sound /saʊnd/

sour /'saʊər/

spicy /'spaɪsi/

starving /'stɑːrvɪŋ/

sweet /swiːt/

to attract /ə'trækt/

to decline /dɪ'klaɪn/

to define /dɪ'faɪn/

to emerge /ɪ'mɜːrʤ/

to own something /oʊn .../

to regret something /rɪ'gret .../

to run something /rʌn .../

to taste /teɪst/

Unit 8

amazed /ə'meɪzd/

amazing /ə'meɪzɪŋ/

ancient /'eɪnʃənt/

body piercing /'bɑːdi ˌpɪrsɪŋ/

bridesmaid /'braɪdzmeɪd/

clowns /klaʊnz/

courage /'kɜːrɪʤ/

demons /'diːmənz/

disappointed /dɪsə'pɔɪnʈɪd/

disappointing /dɪsə'pɔɪnʈɪŋ/

distance /'dɪstəns/

earrings /'ɪrɪŋz/

fascinated /'fæsəneɪʈɪd/

fascinating /'fæsəneɪʈɪŋ/

fashionable /'fæʃənəbəl/

frightened /'fraɪtənd/

index finger /'ɪndeks ˌfɪŋgər/

insulting /ɪn'sʌltɪŋ/

ornaments /'ɔːrnəmənts/

polite /pə'laɪt/

ritual /'rɪʧuəl/

rude /ruːd/

soles /soʊlz/

statue /'stæʧuː/

talents /'tælənts/

thumb /θʌm/

tights /taɪts/

tiring /'taɪrɪŋ/

to cross your legs /ˌkrɑːs jər 'legz/

to fold your arms /ˌfoʊld jər 'ɑːrmz/

to greet someone /griːt .../

to ignore someone /ɪg'nɔːr .../

to imitate /'ɪmɪteɪt/

to insult /ɪn'sʌlt/

to nod /nɑːd/

to point /pɔɪnt/

to point a finger /ˌpɔɪnt ə 'fɪŋgər/

to scare someone /sker .../

to scratch your head /ˌskræʧ jər 'hed/

to shake hands /ˌʃeɪk 'hændz/

to shake your head /ˌʃeɪk jər 'hed/

to sigh /saɪ/

to sink /sɪŋk/

to wave /weɪv/

trendy /'trendi/

unclean /ʌn'kliːn/

worried /'wɜːrid/

worrying /'wɜːriɪŋ/

Unit 9

awards /ə'wɔːrdz/

border /'bɔːrdər/

charity work /'ʧerəʈi ˌwɜːrk/

freedom /'friːdəm/

gold medal /ˌgoʊld 'medəl/

law /lɑː/

rainfall /'reɪnfɔːl/

scenery /'siːnəri/

skateboarder /'skeɪtbɔːrdər/

snow /snoʊ/

snowboarder /'snoʊbɔːrdər/

to be fond of doing something /ˌbi: ˌfɑnd əv 'duːɪŋ .../

to be good at doing something /ˌbi 'gʊd ət 'duːɪŋ .../

to be hopeless at doing something /ˌbi: ˌhoʊpləs ət 'duːɪŋ .../

to be interested in doing something /ˌbi: 'ɪntrɪstɪd ɪn 'duːɪŋ .../

to borrow /'bɑːroʊ/

to compete /kəm'piːt/

to insist on something /ɪn'sɪst ɑːn .../

to look forward to doing something /ˌlʊk ˌfɔːrwərd tə 'duːɪŋ .../

to predict /prɪ'dɪkt/

to steal /stiːl/

to think of doing something /ˌθɪŋk əv 'duɪŋ .../

to win /wɪn/

Unit 10

wooden box /ˌwʊdən 'bɑːks/

bathroom faucets /ˌbæθruːm 'fɑːsɪts/

black market /ˌblæk 'mɑːrkɪt/

comic books /'kɑːmɪk ˌbʊks/

crazy /'kreɪzi/

exotic /ɪg'zɑːʈɪk/

factory /'fæktəri/

fascinated /'fæsɪneɪʈɪd/

fascination /ˌfæsɪ'neɪʃən/

football pictures /'fʊtbɔːl ˌpɪkʧərz/

geology /ʤi'ɑːləʤi/

honeymoon /'hʌnimuːn/

microscope /'maɪkrəskoʊp/

model planes /ˌmɑːdəl 'pleɪnz/

packages /'pækɪʤɪz/

sand /sænd/

seashells /'siːʃelz/

souvenir /suːvə'nɪr/

to collect things /kə'lekt ˌθɪŋz/

to do puzzles /ˌduː 'pʌzəlz/

to fix things /'fɪks ˌθɪŋz/

to get help /ˌget 'help/

to go bird-watching /ˌgoʊ 'bɜːrd ˌwɑːʧɪŋ/

to grow /groʊ/

to join /ʤɔɪn/

to keep /kiːp/

to keep a blog /ˌkiːp ə 'blɑːg/

to lie in the sun /ˌlaɪ ɪn ðə 'sʌn/

to play online games /ˌpleɪ ˌɑːnlaɪn 'geɪmz/

to receive /rɪ'siːv/

to rent /rent/

to search /sɜːrʧ/

to take pictures /ˌteɪk 'pɪkʧərz/

Unit 11

animal testing /'ænɪməl ˌtestɪŋ/

brave /breɪv/

demonstration /ˌdemən'streɪʃən/

determined /dɪˈtɜːrmɪnd/

insensitive /ɪnˈsensət̬ɪv/

inspirational /ˌɪnspəˈreɪʃənəl/

intolerant /ɪnˈtɑːlərənt/

laboratories /læˈbrətɔːriz/

limerick /ˈlɪmərɪk/

long-distance runner /ˌlɑːŋ ˌdɪstənts ˈrʌnər/

miserable /ˈmɪzərəbəl/

negative /ˈnegət̬ɪv/

outgoing /aʊtˈgoʊɪŋ/

patient /ˈpeɪʃənt/

readers /ˈriːdərz/

scared /skerd/

selfish /ˈselfɪʃ/

stupid /ˈstuːpɪd/

syllable /ˈsɪləbəl/

to accept /əkˈsept/

to appreciate /əˈpriːʃieɪt/

to bully /ˈbʊli/

to calm down /kɑːm ˈdaʊn/

to cheer someone up /tʃɪr … ˈʌp/

to crash /kræʃ/

to figure things out /ˌfɪgjər θɪŋz ˈaʊt/

to fit in /fɪt ˈɪn/

to get angry /ˌget ˈæŋgri/

to get into fights /ˌget ɪntə ˈfaɪts/

to hang out with someone /ˌhæŋ ˈaʊt wɪð …/

to hate /heɪt/

to judge /dʒʌdʒ/

to laugh at someone /ˈlɑːf ət …/

to pick on someone /ˈpɪk ɑːn …/

to share /ʃer/

to spread lies /ˌspred ˈlaɪz/

to take a long time /ˌteɪk ə ˌlɑːŋ ˈtaɪm/

to tell someone off /tel … ˈɑːf/

to treat /triːt/

to whisper /ˈwɪspər/

tolerant /ˈtɑːlərənt/

unadventurous /ˌʌnədˈventʃərəs/

Unit 12

chemicals /ˈkemɪkəlz/

court /kɔːrt/

daybreak /ˈdeɪbreɪk/

fair price /ˌfer ˈpraɪs/

farm /fɑːrm/

fixed price /ˌfɪkst ˈpraɪs/

furious /ˈfjʊriəs/

guard /gɑːrd/

mine /maɪn/

pesticides /ˈpestəsaɪdz/

prison /ˈprɪzən/

shade /ʃeɪd/

soup /suːp/

terrified /ˈterəfaɪd/

to be fair/unfair /ˌbi ˈfer, ʌnˈfer/

to beat someone /biːt …/

to care about /ˈker əˌbaʊt/

to cheat /tʃiːt/

to dig /dɪg/

to do experiments /ˌduː ɪkˈsperəmənts/

to earn money /ˌɜːrn ˈmʌni/

to fail a test /ˌfeɪl ə ˈtest/

to find /faɪnd/

to go to prison /ˌgoʊ tə ˈprɪzən/

to grow food /ˌgroʊ ˈfuːd/

to have a crash /ˌhæv ə ˈkræʃ/

to hear /hɪr/

to knock on the door /ˌnɑːk ɑːn ðə ˈdɔːr/

to lend /lend/

to pick something up /pɪk … ˈʌp/

to shout /ʃaʊt/

to steal /stiːl/

to store things /ˈstɔːr ˌθɪŋz/

to study hard /ˌstʌdi ˈhɑːrd/

to throw /θroʊ/

to turn around /tɜːrn əˈraʊnd/

to worry about something /ˈwɜːri əˌbaʊt …/

warehouse /ˈwerhaʊs/

Pronunciation guide

Vowels

/iː/	real, screen
/ɪ/	dish, sit
/i/	funny
/e/	chess, bed
/æ/	bad, taxi
/ʌ/	must, done
/ʊ/	good, full
/uː/	choose, view
/ə/	dramatic, the
/ɑː/	stop, opera
/ɔː/	saw, daughter

Vowels + /r/

/ɜːr/	first, shirt
/ɑːr/	car
/ɔːr/	horse
/er/	their
/ʊr/	tourist
/ɪr/	ear
/ər/	teacher

Diphthongs

/eɪ/	play, train
/aɪ/	ice, night
/ɔɪ/	employer, noisy
/aʊ/	house, download
/oʊ/	no, window

Consonants

/p/	push
/b/	bank
/t/	time
/ʈ/	butter
/d/	diary
/k/	carpet
/g/	big
/f/	surf
/v/	very
/θ/	thin
/ð/	that
/s/	sit
/z/	zero
/ʃ/	shine
/ʒ/	measure
/h/	hot
/w/	water
/tʃ/	chair
/dʒ/	joke
/m/	more
/n/	snow
/ŋ/	sing
/r/	ring
/l/	small
/j/	you

CAMBRIDGE UNIVERSITY PRESS
www.cambridge.org/elt

HELBLING LANGUAGES
www.helblinglanguages.com

American MORE! 4 Student's Book
by Herbert Puchta & Jeff Stranks
with G. Gerngross C. Holzmann P. Lewis-Jones

© Cambridge University Press and Helbling Languages 2010
(MORE! was originally published by Helbling Languages © Helbling Languages 2006)

Printed in Italy by L.E.G.O. S.p.A.

ISBN 978-0-521-17159-5   American MORE! 4 Student's Book with interactive CD-ROM
ISBN 978-0-521-17162-5   American MORE! 4 Workbook with Audio CD
ISBN 978-0-521-17163-2   American MORE! 4 Teacher's Book
ISBN 978-0-521-17165-6   American MORE! 4 Teacher's Resource Pack with Testbuilder CD-ROM/Audio CD
ISBN 978-0-521-17166-3   American MORE! 4 Class Audio CDs
ISBN 978-0-521-17169-4   American MORE! 4 Extra Practice Book
ISBN 978-0-521-17170-0   American MORE! 4 DVD (NTSC)

The authors would like to thank those people who have made significant contributions toward the final form of American MORE!

Oonagh Wade and Rosamund Cantalamessa for their expertise in working on the manuscripts, their useful suggestions for improvement, and the support we got from them.

Lucia Astuti and Markus Spielmann, Helbling Languages, Ron Ragsdale and James Dingle, Cambridge University Press, for their dedication to the project and innovative publishing vision.

Our designers—Amanda Hockin, Greg Sweetnam, Quantico, Craig Cornell, and Niels Gyde—for their imaginative layouts and stimulating creativity. Also, our artwork assistants, Francesca Gironi and Elisa Pasqualini, for their dedicated work.

The publishers would like to thank the following for their kind permission to reproduce the following photographs and other copyright material:

Alamy p9 (log rolling contest), p10 (Bombonera Stadium; sack race), p12 (Pilgrims), p35 (writer), p37, p45 (CD: Food Icon; pizza), p52 (whale), p54 (Mardy Fish), p56 (tennis tournament, school fair), p62 (Boston marathon), p66 (CD: Food Icon; baked potato), p70 (CD: Food Icons; CD: Ultimate Food), p72, p73, p80, p86, p93, p96 (mending bicycle; making models), p114, p116 (prison warden); **Associated Press** p73 (Moby; Menudo; Bon Jovi); from *A Step from Heaven*, by An Na. Copyright © 2001 by An Na. Published by Front Street, an imprint of **Boyds Mills Press**. Reprinted by permission, p46; **Dreamstime** p60, p70 (children), p75 (excited girl), p89, p90 (Shakira), p96 (Blogger), p99 (Olympics Collector Pins), p122; **Getty Images** p60 (logo of Wimbledon), p86 (Cars); **The International Sand Collectors Society, Nick D'Errico** ISCS/PG Director p94; ©**Istockphoto** p6 (shoes), p10 (volleyball; basketball), p11, p34 (Philip), p35 (farmer), p40, p49, p52 (salmon), p53 (Arctic terns), p59, p62 (New York City marathon), p63, p71 (New York City), p75 (girl yawning, disappointed boy), p76 (girls cross legs), p91, p103,

p105 (girl with pets), p109, p116 (miner; aerobics teacher), p123; **Jupiterimages** p9 (fish), p35 (policeman), p39, p43 (George); **David Loftus** p69 (Jamie Oliver); © 2004 **Mojave Aerospace Ventures, LLC.** SpaceShipOne®, A Paul G. AllenProject, p19 (SpaceShipOne); **NASA, NSSDC** p14; **Penguin Group Ltd** front cover of *Half Moon Investigations* by Eoin Colfer (Puffin 2006) p46; Cover from *Crocodile Tears* by Anthony Horowitz. Used by permission of Philomel Books, a division of **Penguin Young Readers Group** p49; **Planet Space** p19 (Canadian Arrow); **Public domain**/ph Helbling Languages p79 (Sir Walter Ralegh), jacket cover from *The Curious Incident Of The Dog In The Night-Time* by Mark Haddon. Used by permission of Doubleday, a division of **Random House, Inc.** p46; book cover of *The Lost Art* by Simon Morden, reprinted by permission of **The Random House Group Ltd** p46; **Reuters** p30; **Shutterstock** p6, p9 (street luge), p10 (football; baseball), p12, p14 (spaceship top left), p26, p31, p32, p33, p34 (Mandy), p35, p37 (boy, ballet dancer, army reserve officers), p43 (omelet), p45, p53, p54 (Sheri), p56, p59 (concert), p63 (girl), p66, p70 (spinach; milk; hot dog; cabbage; coffee; pineapple; hamburger; chocolate), p71, p74 (boy no. 1), p75 (bored boy; frightened boy), p76 (girl waving; girl with arms folded; men shake hands; doctor scratches head), p79 (piercing), p82, p85, p86 (Angelina Jolie), p89 (Winona Ryder), p90, p92, p94 (sand), p96, p99, p102, p105, p116; **Space Today Online** p19 (da Vinci Wild Fire); **United States Library of Congress** p13; **Universal Music Group** p86 (Ta-Dah); **Veer** p42; **Warner Music Group** p86 (Crazy); **Courtesy of The White House** p90 (Barack Obama); **Wikimedia Commons** p12 (Mayflower), p22, p86 (Beyoncé, Brad Pitt), p90 (Steven Spielberg).

The publishers would like to thank the following illustrators:
Roberto Battestini, Pietro Dichiara, Michele Farella, Björn Pertoft, Lucilla Stellato.

The publishers would like to thank the following for their assistance with commissioned photography:
David Tolley Ltd. p104; Ed-Imaging pp4, 24, 44, 64, 84; Studio Antonietti pp15, 74, 75, 76, 77, 99 (pens; tea bags).